Cycle Sport

Peter Konopka

Cycle Sport

Equipment, Technique and Training

The Crowood Press

First published in 1989 by
The Crowood Press
Ramsbury, Marlborough,
Wiltshire SN8 2HE

English translation © The Crowood
Press 1989

Translated by Michael and Rita
Matthews

**British Library Cataloguing in
Publication Data**

Konopka, Peter
    Cycle sport.
    1. Bicycle racing & bicycle touring
    – Manuals
    I. Title   II. Radsport. *English*
    796.6'2

    ISBN 1 85223 280 3

Title of the original German edition:
Radsport
© 1988 Verlagsgesellschaft mbH,
MÜNCHEN

Illustrations

Birkner: p. 118
Brügelmann-Radsport: pp. 42, 60
Heckmair: p. 18
Kahlich: pp. 2/3, 6 (3), 7 (3), 8/9, 10, 11,
15, 16, 17 (3), 18 (2), 20, 21, 22 (2),
27 (2), 28, 29 (2), 31, 35 (2), 36, 37,
38 (2), 39 (4), 40, 44 (2), 46 (5), 47
(12), 48 (2), 49 (9), 50 (6), 51 (4), 52/53,
54 (3), 55 (2), 56 (3), 57 (2), 58 (5), 59
(2), 60, 61, 62 (2), 63, 64 (2), 65, 69, 73,
75, 76, 77, 78 (2), 79, 80, 83, 84, 85 (2),
86/87, 91, 93, 95, 99, 103, 107, 111,
124/125, 127, 130, 131, 133, 134, 135,
136, 138/139, 144, 147, 148, 149,
150/151, 154/155, 159
Konopka: pp. 6, 16, 20, 22, 25, 26, 28,
29, 30, 34(3), 36, 39, 40, 42, 43(3), 44,
45, 55, 56, 114/115 (12), 116/117 (12),
120/121 (12), 123, 140
Penazzo: p. 41
Schuschke/Öttinger: pp. 18/19
Vespa GmbH: pp. 23, 39
Witek: p. 143

The illustrations on pages 12, 13 and 14
were provided by W. Gronen. The
use of the illustrations on pages 46–51
was kindly authorised by Atlas Verlag
und Werbung GmbH.
Title-page photograph: Peter Witek
Graphics: Barbara von Damnitz
Layout: Anton Walter

Dr Peter Konopka (born in 1940)
studied medicine at the universities of
Erlangen, Tübingen and Munich and
graduated from the University of
Munich as a pathologist. He subsequently gained experience in sports
medicine as an assistant to the medical
officer at Bayern Munich FC before
dedicating the following years to general practice. Since 1977 he has been
employed as a senior physician in
Augsburg.

He has always shown particular interest in the theory of 'health through
exercise and good nutrition' and so it is
not surprising that his interests in sport
and medicine led him to take the position of team doctor for the BDR (German National Cycling Federation). (He
also became a member of the Society
of Bavarian Doctors.)

He has published numerous books,
brochures and articles, mainly concerned with nutrition and training, and
regularly contributes to the German
cycling magazine, *Radmagazin Tour.*
Dr Konopka is himself an active cyclist
and has won several important cycling
events. He still participates in veteran
events today for, as he himself states,
'Once you are hooked on cycle races,
you cannot help but participate in
them.'

Typeset by Inforum Typesetting
Printed in Spain by Graficas Estella, S.A. (Navarra)

At some time in our life we all experience the fun and enjoyment of riding a bike. Indeed enjoyment is what cycling is all about, whether it be short rides in the country with the family, club runs and competitions, or aiming for international success as an amateur or professional. In reaching the top echelon of world-class professional racing, I have progressed through all the other categories and enjoyed every one on the way. Gaining top professional victories is now my job but enjoying cycling is still most important.

Whether you are just a weekend cyclist or a determined competitor aiming for the top, there is something to be learned from the contents of Dr Konopka's book. Every area of technical value is covered, with explicit, detailed articles on diet, medicine, equipment, training and competition – and these are complemented by quality illustrations and precise technical data. Without doubt, the knowledge and experience gained by Dr Konopka throughout his years involved in cycle sport are combined to make this one of the most detailed books written on the sport.

As a young rider I became conscious of the importance of cycle maintenance, correct diet and food, in addition to the necessary training and tactical racing knowledge. This book describes in detail all aspects of cycling and provides the modern-day cyclist with the information required for both enjoyment and success.

In my present-day racing it is even more important to prepare correctly, especially when such races as the *Tour de France* are the objectives; the knowledge and experience of Dr Konopka highlights all the important areas involved. During the twenty-four days of the *Tour* almost every situation referred to in the pages of this book will arise. Riding style may need to be adjusted during the mountain stage as it will differ from the style for those stages on the flat.

Eating and drinking during the race is as important as before and after – constant medical checks are also carried out during a race of this duration. The maintenance of the bicycles is performed by the mechanics and the massage, diet and medical side is the responsibility of the *soigneur*. All these factors are important to every cyclist, but to varying degrees; the study of these aspects in Dr Konopka's book will assist and provide the appropriate information as necessary.

As a reference book for enjoyable and successful cycling this is a must. It is the type of book that will always provide some new information whenever you pick it up. The knowledge and experience of Dr Konopka is passed on in a way which can only benefit the cyclist, regardless of the category to which he may belong.

Malcolm Elliott
1989

Contents

Contents

Regeneration

Diet

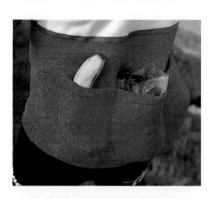

Competition

Cycling and Medicine

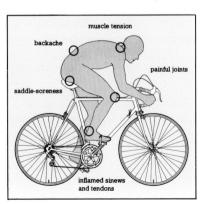

muscle tension

backache

painful joints

saddle-soreness

inflamed sinews and tendons

Preface

When I was asked to serve as a doctor for the German national team of road-racing cyclists in the early 1970s I did not realise how much cycling would dominate and enrich my life. In my youth I had participated in some cycle races but my involvement was too short to enable me to discover the secrets of cycling without some kind of instruction. Fortunately, my friend Karl Ziegler, who was then the national coach for the road and cross-country cyclists, has initiated me into these secrets during our long years of working together. Rudi Altig, my favourite cyclist during my youth, has also shared his experiences as a professional racing cyclist. Practical experience of this kind is immensely valuable as it cannot be learned from a book. Karl Link, the national coach, also helped me to get closer to track training.

Serving as a doctor for the national team spurred me on to explore all kinds of new activities; I began cycle training again, this time participating in veterans' races, lapping everything up and becoming more fascinated with cycling day by day. I have been able to gain experience both as a doctor and as a cyclist while serving at world championships, the Olympic Games, stage races and training camps throughout Europe, Africa and South America, for which I am eternally grateful to the *Bund Deutscher Radfahrer* (German National Cycling Federation).

I was not only fascinated by the medical aspect of cycle sport, but by everything connected with it; the secret of the speed of pedalling; the build-up of training; strengthening of the defence mechanism of the body; recuperation; healthy living and nutrition – and by cycle equipment and the idea of the bicycle as a sports instrument. I have learned a great deal about this from watching the very able and reliable mechanics of the German national team, Manfred Otte and Klaus Lauer.

While recording my experiences I realised how difficult it can be to describe – particularly in detail – objects and activities which seem so simple. My friends Peter Krauss, coach of RSG Augsberg, and Willi Singer, an ex-professional cyclist, have often helped me out with this problem.

Karl Ziegler told me of a computer 'buff' called Wolfgang Gronen just at the right moment (when I was busy writing about the bicycle and cycling). He, too, offered much help.

I learned from numerous cyclists around the world just how far cycling allows us to improve the quality of our life – and especially so nowadays. On more than one occasion I have witnessed people 'taking their destiny into their own hands' and conquering illnesses *by cycling*. For a doctor this is more satisfying than simply prescribing medicines.

The bicycle has something to offer everyone, but it is more complicated than a pair of running shoes or a tennis racquet. The biological machine (the human being) and the mechanical machine (the bicycle) have to work together in harmony if the best results are to be achieved.

This book has grown out of experiences which experts have shared with me and which I myself have found to be effective while treating cyclists in

Cycling in the country – an ideal opportunity for relaxation.

my surgery. I hope that this book will guide the reader into the wonderful world of cycling – so that he or she may benefit from cycling as I have.

Dr Peter Konopka.

Cycling for Leisure and Relaxation

Today's increase in motoring, technology and automation has led to a widespread lack of exercise amongst most people. This is a major cause of disease in the West. Human beings are, like all other living creatures, dependent upon the law of nature which means that both the hereditary structure and function of our organs and also the quality and quantity of the demand we make on them affect our health – in other words everyone can improve the efficiency and function of their organs and their entire body by suitable exercise, irrespective of age. This is a very encouraging scientific discovery! Insufficient exercise is unnatural and promotes illness, but fortunately it is not necessary to take up strenuous sport in order to alleviate the consequences of insufficient exercise. Nervous tension and stress, both common complaints today, can also be overcome by taking exercise; the most beneficial sports are those which improve stamina. Cycling is one of these, and is also rather special.

One very noticeable advantage of cycling as a leisure activity is that your body-weight is carried by the saddle. This is particularly useful for overweight and under-trained cyclists since neither joints nor tendons will suffer unusual strain, even after many hours cycling. People suffering from weak joints or various forms of arthritis are able to be active cyclists even when it is impossible for them to go walking, as the intensity of effort is easily controlled on a bicycle. Indeed cycling, when practised to varying extents, is suitable for all age ranges. Moreover, taking exercise in fresh air means a strengthening of the immune system of the body.

Consideration should also be given to the aesthetics of the body, which seem to be particularly important to the ever increasing number of female cyclists. The wind gives the skin a healthy glow, and fat which is located at the top of the legs and round the hips simply melts away like butter in the sun. Ideally you should be active throughout the year if the benefits from exercise are to be maximised – and this is possible with the bicycle, although it would be advisable to go for a run instead when snow is lying on the ground. Cycling is a particularly suitable sport for introducing inactive people to the pleasures of taking exercise and to introduce them to other kinds of sport.

Regular physical activity brings about physical and mental well-being, promotes relaxation and reduces undesirable weight gain.

School-age children also benefit from cycling because it promotes the development of body and mind, and lessens aggression so that a child's concentration improves. Good health and improved resistance to illness conveys a new feeling of life.

There is no reason why leisure cycling cannot become a discovery sport – entire families can cycle in groups, and if the bicycles are equipped with saddlebags (or you use a mountain-bike), places inaccessible by car will suddenly be there to be explored.

Thousands of keen cyclists have stated that it is well worthwhile investing in a good-quality bicycle, and to look after it with great care. It might even be useful to purchase a second cycle for special events.

Competitive and Professional Cycling

Road-racing cyclists have a special position in various types of endurance sport. In fact, they could be labelled 'the kings of the athletes' as they are more powerful than other sportspeople. Cyclists competing in the *Tour de France* must endure hard racing for

Introduction

many hours on end, day after day, over a period of three weeks. Indeed, tests have shown that road-racing cyclists have more strength and stamina than any other kind of athlete – they need the stamina of the marathon runner, the speed of the sprinter and the power of the rower. Road-racing cyclists have the ability to take in the largest possible amount of oxygen per kilogram of body-weight and they also have the largest heart volume and lung capacity.

The giants of the road cover a distance between 20,000 and 40,000km every year – between three and six million rotations of the pedals – without joint complaints requiring medical treatment. Indeed cycling is a good example of how the human body is able to adjust to different situations – an interesting phenomenon nowadays when so many people suffer from lack of exercise.

Some aspects of cycling are of interest not only to cyclists but also to other athletes. These aspects include: the operation of the digestive system under pressure; the food and the care needed when the body is under maximum strain; the results of a sudden relief from strain and stress after racing; the differing abilities of women and men to adjust to these conditions; and the problems arising from constant stress associated with stage-racing.

Cycling looks so simple, but even today there are still secrets to be learned about the way in which cyclists can improve their performance. There is always the difficult choice between power and stamina when in training and in competition, and questions such as 'Which gear should I use?' and 'How fast should I pedal?' often seem to crop up. New research into muscle structure and metabolism help support scientifically the experiences of past racing cyclists. One of the aims of this book is to bring these previous experiences into harmony with modern scientific knowledge and so optimise the training process. 'Optimised training' means achieving the best possible results over the shortest period of time and to achieve this it is important to be well informed and knowledgeable about both cycling and training, that is to know enough to do the right thing.

The pack charges forward, wheel against wheel, handlebar against handlebar.

Cycling as Rehabilitation Training

Athletes from all sports and disciplines can begin training on a bicycle soon after an injury or operation and before they embark on normal training for their own sport – for example, cycling is the best way to train after an operation to an injured cartilage and so may prove invaluable to a runner. Cycle training can soon begin and this will help in the recovery of the joint.

Cycling as Subsidiary and Stamina Training

Many other athletes from a variety of different disciplines – such as skiers, hockey players, tennis players (Ivan Lendl owns eight racing cycles) and racing drivers – use cycling during the winter or off season months in order to improve their stamina.

Cycling: Fascination and Enthusiasm

The special fascination of cycling derives from the harmony of the human body (the biological machine) and the bicycle (the technical machine). People who have developed the feeling for this harmony will become addicted cyclists and never turn back. In order to enjoy cycling fully you must understand two things; yourself and the bicycle. You will soon notice that cycling makes physical and mental demands, of which the beginner may be quite unaware. I

More and more athletes take to cycling as a recreational sport – including rally world champion Walter Roehrl (centre) and cross-country cycling world champion Klaus-Peter Thaler.

hope that this book will awaken a love and enthusiasm for cycling, and if so, you will not be alone. You will be joining other people, famous inventors, artists, academics, politicians, barons and kings, all of whom were fascinated with the invention of the bicycle, and indeed some contributed to its invention.

With this book you should learn everything there is to know about cycling and the bicycle. The bicycle is a reliable piece of sports equipment which will serve its owner for many years – through thick and thin – and which can encourage good health and plenty of exercise for a whole lifetime.

The History of Cycling and the Bicycle

The bicycle is arguably one of the most amazing of inventions. There is nothing remotely comparable in nature since it would be impossible for a 'living' wheel (made up of cells and constantly turning around an axle) to gain any nourishment. Indeed it is impossible to imagine technology without the wheel; world history would have developed very differently without it.

Originally the wheel was a disc constructed of two or three wooden pieces, fixed at the axle, and as such was never anything more sophisticated than a cart-wheel. The oldest existing cart can be traced back over 5,000 years and cart-wheels with spokes are reported to have been used in Mesopotamia 4,000 years ago. However, it is

Introduction

said that the Chinese used wheels with spokes over 6,000 years ago.

Nobody came up with the idea of placing one wheel behind the other and using them for transport, rather than the obvious system of having two wheels next to each other. This idea, which by now is so obvious, was then unimaginable since it was not realised that rotating wheels have a stabilising effect. Simple types of wheel, connected with a form of spindle, can be found in old Egyptian and Chinese drawings dating back to 1300 BC. In fact, for at least 3,000 years, people have been preoccupied with the idea of combining a piece of technical equipment with human energy in order to become mobile.

The history of the bicycle itself starts in the year 1818 when Carl Friedrich Christian Ludwig Baron Drais von Sauerbronn applied for a patent on his steerable walking bicycle, later called the 'Draisine' in his honour.

Nobody could have anticipated that the bicycle would become known as 'the little man's car' and that its popularity would increase so phenomenally. It is about 170 years since the Baden forestry commissioner dared to step out into the road of Karlsruhe with his two-wheeled cart, built solely for his own enjoyment. People laughed and satirists ridiculed him when the inventor rolled through the streets with his 'running machine'.

*Racing machine
(Michauline)
dating from 1869.*

The machine was made from a wooden frame with two wooden wheels, which he mobilised by 'running' with it. A Karlsruhe newspaper reported that he covered a distance – which had taken a post coach four hours – in a quarter of the time. A me-

chanic named Mylius then constructed a bicycle in around 1845 which was driven by a crank (push-and-tread motion) fixed to the front wheel. Philipp Moritz Fischer (a musical instrument maker from Schweinfurt) built a similar bicycle with a crank in 1853, but the bicycle experienced its first proper breakthrough when the French mechanic Pierre Michaux showed his invention of a cranked bicycle, which he called his 'Velociped', at a world exhibition in 1897. It was subsequently called a 'Michauline' in his honour.

With each new design, the front wheel of the bicycle grew constantly larger since it was used as the driving wheel and the cyclist wanted to cover the maximum distance with one revolution of the pedals. This explains the de-

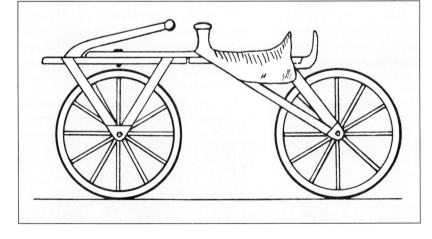

*Draisine: a drawing taken from the contract
between the Baron Drais and the ministry of
Baden (1818).*

son invented a bicycle with a chain leading to the rear wheel in 1879. Solid rubber tyres had been used since 1869, but these were replaced by pneumatic tyres in 1888 – devised by Scotsman John Boyd Dunlop. The wheel hub was invented by the German Ernst Sachs at the turn of the century, and then came the invention of the rear brakes. By now there was no stopping the growing popularity of cycling. The bicycle had been born.

Competing against others is a natural human desire and the first competition on Draisines took place in Paris in 1819,

only two years after the invention of these 'running bicycles'. The first road race was organised in Amiens in 1865, but only over a distance of 500 metres. The first international event took place in 1869, and covered the route between Paris and Rouen (130km). Interestingly, women participated in this event – surprising for such an early date. A race over the Alps to Milan in Italy is also reported to have taken place in 1880 and a road race of 87km was one of the disciplines in the first Olympic games in 1896. Since 1868 in England and 1882 in Germany, track

B. Zierfuß, Berlin, German champion of 1893 with his penny farthing.

velopment of the penny farthing – the front wheel had become as large as was feasible, while the rear wheel had become as small as was feasible. The Parisian mechanic, Victor Renard, constructed a penny farthing with a front wheel measuring three metres (three and a half feet) in diameter and weighing sixty-five kilograms! It is easy to understand how bicycles of this dimension led to dangerous falls. So the penny farthing soon lost its popularity, its inventor dying in his workshop in 1893.

Inventors from a variety of different countries were then instrumental in the further development of the bicycle. The first machine equipped with cranks fitted on the rear wheel was invented by André Guilmet in 1868. W. A. Cowper constructed a bicycle with iron spokes in 1870, and J. Truffauts invented the iron rim. Undoubtedly the greatest advance came when H. J. Law-

Introduction

G. P. Mills, first winner of the Bordeaux–Paris race in 1891.

race from Paris to Roubaix, when following a 'car' in 1899. The two Wright brothers, Orville and Wilbur, who achieved the first successful manned flight, were road and track racing cyclists and owned a bicycle shop in which they made their own machines.

Stage-racing has also been influential in the history of European cycling. The most famous race is, of course, the *Tour de France*, founded by the journalist Henri Desgranges in 1903. It was his aim to offer the French a magnificent spectacle during the hottest month of the year, 'when the cows bellow with thirst in the field, and the grass withers at the roadside'. In his leading article for the sports magazine *L'auto*, dated 1 July 1903, he wrote '*L'auto* launches today – with innovation, courage and a zest as great as that with which Emile Zola endows his peasants in his novel *La Terre* – the greatest race in the world with the most magnificent and courageous of all athletes. While covering the distance of 2,400km they will meet astonished onlookers who will feel ashamed of their own comfort and who will be awakened by the power and the endless energy of these outstanding sportsmen.' The popularity of long cycle races is rooted deep in every nation with an interest in cycling.

cycle racing has existed, and in 1891 in New York the first six-day event was staged, Europe holding its first such competition in 1909 in Berlin.

By this time cycling was a royal sport; not only were mechanics, technicians, engineers and watchmakers fascinated with the bicycle, but emperors, kings and royal subjects were also participating in the increasingly popular sport.

Emperor Napoleon III donated a gold medal to the winner of a road-race in 1868, and Emperor Wilhelm I also donated a trophy for penny farthing races – from that day on the race for the 'Emperor's prize' was an annual event. The five German von Opel

brothers drew attention to themselves when, in succession, they each won the Hessen championships race. One of the brothers, Ludwig von Opel, had been the runner-up in the world sprint event championship in Vienna in 1898.

Artists such as Henri de Toulouse-Lautrec, Claude Monet, Pablo Picasso, Max Ernst and numerous others were also aware of the bicycle (if not keen cyclists) as they all included it in their works, so bestowing on it an immortality. Indeed there were many influential people involved with the development of the bicycle; the Frenchman Albert Champion (who invented the sparking-plug that still carries his name) won the first classic road

Famous Racing Cyclists

It is impossible to list every famous racing cyclist. A selection will always be subjective, although it must, of course, be a selection which uses as its criteria for inclusion the success of the cycling champions. Some had easier times than others, largely dependent upon whether or not fellow competitors were of a similar ability to the champions themselves.

Not only did they have to prove themselves in stage-races such as the

Tour de France, but also in other classic races such as the *Giro d'Italia*, the *Tour de Suisse*, the road-racing world championships and other traditional great events. So the history of cycling has recorded great names such as Gino Bartali, Fausto Coppi, Felice Gimondi, Francesco Moser and Guiseppe Saronni from Italy, Louison Bobet, Jacques Anquetil, Bernard Hinault and Raymond Poulidor from France, Rik van Steenbergen, Rik von Looy and the great Eddy Merckx from Belgium, Jan Janssen from Holland, and Ferdi Kubler and Hugo Koblet from Switzerland.

The best German racing cyclists after the Second World War were definitely Rudi Altig, Hennes Junkermann and Rolf Wolfshohl. Klaus-Peter Thaler, Dietrich Thurau and Gregor Braun were also very successful and Rolf Golz, Hartmut Boelz and Raimund Dietzen are well-known names of today.

Europe is, as it always has been, the El Dorado of the road-racing cyclist. Road-racing cyclists from countries in which the sport is not quite as important as in the rest of Europe have increasingly found their way to the top – riders such as Sean Kelly and Stephen Roche from Ireland, as well as Phil Anderson from Australia and Greg Lemond from America (who is less well-known in his own country than in Europe).

Some racing cyclists were so popular during their time that they have been depicted on postage stamps, for instance Bartali, Kubler, Bobet, Janssen, Anquetil, Gimondi and Merckx have all appeared on stamps. Indeed roads, places and stadiums have been named after racing cyclists such as Robel, Timoner, Moeskops and Linart. In cycling, supremacy undoubtedly belongs to the countries of Italy, France, Belgium, Holland and Switzerland. The passion for cycling runs deeper in these countries – and it is this passion that turns ordinary human beings into competitive racing cyclists.

The leading pack attacking on the summit during the Tour de Suisse *(leading, on the right, Greg Lemond, winner of the* Tour de France*).*

Equipment

The Right Cycle for the Right Purpose

When purchasing a bicycle it is, of course, important to bear in mind what you will use it for. Perhaps the machine you already own is sufficient for your purposes? It is usually the type of cycling that you intend to undertake that determines the type of bicycle, and not vice versa. Making this choice will cause you to realise the number of ways in which a bicycle can be used, and how it opens up new opportunities. Why not purchase a second or third cycle in the same way that others purchase two or even three motor cars?

A touring sports bicycle with mudguards, chain-guards, luggage carrier and lights.

The Bicycle for the Adventurous

Cycling can bring about a very unfamiliar feeling in today's motorised world – the feeling of covering remarkably long distances with little effort and quite speedily using nothing more than your own physical energy. You can properly take in the atmosphere of the countryside (unlike travelling by car) and are surprised to discover how fresh the air is beyond the towns and cities. Some people even claim that you can 'smell' the countryside. To be sure, you can get much closer to nature, can bring yourself into accord with her and experience the rhythm of the seasons much more intensively – if you have a bicycle. The more you forget the actual process of cycling, the more you can enjoy the surroundings.

Accordingly, it is important to purchase a proper touring bicycle or even a modern lightweight touring/sports bicycle. Speeds will be higher when touring than in town and winds will be stronger out in the open countryside, so the position on a touring bicycle will be slightly lower than on a normal, everyday cycle. Hub gears are sufficient for touring in the countryside, but the difference from one gear to the next is so marked that it is advantageous to be able to use gears in between the usual three available with hub gears – and so, if possible, you should purchase a bicycle with five or six gears (which will make touring more enjoyable). The gears are not designed to bring about speed, but to make pedalling easier, even in rough countryside – the only way to maximise the enjoyment of what is a very healthy pastime; touring.

The touring bicycle has already been equipped with some special features:

1. Efficient calliper or hub-brakes, needed because of the increased speed and load.
2. Five or six speed freewheel.

The bicycle turns nature into an experience.

All you need do to have ten or twelve-speed gears is to double the front chainwheel as this, multiplied by the number of cogs on the freewheel (five or six) gives the total number of gears available. However, this is only theoretical since in practice only six or eight gears are available, due to increased chainline. (*See also* page 33.)

Saddles are no longer designed simply to be comfortable but as an aid to pedalling. Instead of sitting on the backside, you should actually sit on the pelvic bones – which are the same in everyone – so a narrow saddle is suitable even for larger cyclists. The tip of the saddle should not be too wide or it will prevent you from adopting a good cycling style with a narrow leg movement (without rubbing the top of the thigh against the tip of the saddle).

Straight, comfortable handlebars are quite adequate on a touring bicycle; indeed curved handlebars may be of no benefit. Even racing cyclists do not use the low position on the curved bars all the time. Certainly there is no need to force yourself into an uncomfortable riding position while touring simply to give the impression of being a racing cyclist – breathing would be impaired and the style would not be relaxed. Indeed such a posture can be dangerous as you are only able to look five metres (five yards) or so ahead and may be travelling at quite a high speed. A large number of accidents have occurred because of this, not to mention the tension that it causes the shoulder muscles.

It is worth considering the use of toe-clips on the pedals of a touring machine as they allow you more grip on the pedals, so making it easier to turn them (*see also* page 70).

People who wish to undertake long journeys by bicycle will probably need a saddlebag. It is quite surprising just how much luggage can be loaded on to a bicycle, but you should remember that the handling of the cycle will be affected, especially when cornering. The benefits of such rides, though, are immense – it is really exciting to leave

The mountain-bike: a special bicycle for every type of terrain.

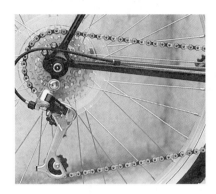

Gears with long levers to accommodate a large number of gears.

Three chainwheels offer the opportunity of cycling in very low gears in rough terrain.

the usual roads behind and ride across countryside inaccessible to the motor car.

You can gain this 'off-road experience' on a touring bicycle, but even better is the purpose-built mountain bike now widely available. Mountain-bike holidays have now become possible – to the amazement of people walking hill and mountain paths, who are stunned by the appearance a cyclist. This terrain is possible on a mountain bike which has been developed with special features with this type of exploration in mind. One of these features is the wide, thick tyres giving a good grip on both soft and hard surfaces. The ultra-low gearing makes it

possible to conquer unbelievably steep climbs.

The cycle has a triple chainwheel on the front, and a five- or six-speed freewheel on the rear wheel, giving fifteen- or eighteen-speed gearing with perhaps even a ratio of 1 : 1 (an equal number of teeth on both front and rear gear cogs). Some models are equipped with asymmetrical (oval) chainwheels, which, it is claimed, assist in the upward movement of the pedals, overcoming the 'top dead centre'.

Overleaf: exhilarating outdoor experiences with a mountain bike, whether in the Himalayas or at home.

Equipment

BMX races require great skill and fitness.

The Bicycle as a Piece of Sports Equipment

Once you have familiarised yourself with any kind of bicycle, you will realise that it is an ideal piece of sports equipment. It is ideal both for people in stressful jobs who otherwise would take little exercise, and also for athletes of all sporting disciplines who need to increase their stamina so that their performance may be improved. Moreover, it is now common knowledge that every athlete needs a certain amount of stamina for good performance and recovery, whether they be tennis, squash or football players or winter athletes wishing to improve their training schedule during the summer months. In each case cycling will provide an excellent means of gaining stamina. Those whose favourite sport is cycling will, of course, also have the opportunity to develop fully their personality.

A piece of sports equipment which can meet these demands must have special qualities. The elite of all cycles is the racing bicycle or, as some call it, the racing machine.

In cycling, performance is dependent upon the interaction between the

Wide, robust handlebars are typical of a mountain bike, as are the tough, efficient, cantilever brakes. The gear-levers are positioned on the handlebars, so that both hands can be used to control the cycle even when changing gear. The saddle height can be quickly changed via a quick-release lever to maintain balance when covering different types of terrain. Another characteristic feature of the mountain bike is that it is very solid, not only in the construction of its frame, but also its wheels and its other major components, all of which are substantially made. It is this tough construction that makes mountain bikes so fascinating and causes people to buy one as a second bicycle – for daily use and for touring. The cycle can then be equipped with lights, mudguards and panniers front and rear.

BMX bicycles can be considered as a small version of a mountain bike and indeed, children are particularly fond of them. The BMX cycle is almost as tough and indestructable as its larger brother as it, too, is normally made with good quality components. However, the BMX is unsuitable for touring because of its low gear ratio but it is still and ideal piece of sport or leisure

equipment for children and simultaneously satisfies two goals; children get pleasure and exercise from cycling and they also learn how to handle a bicycle safely.

The racing bicycle – the perfect piece of sports equipment.

rider and the racing bicycle and so one has to match the other as exactly as possible – you will ride many thousands of kilometres uphill and downhill and in all kinds of weather. Because it is so important that the racing bicycle matches its rider, you should buy the cycle from a specialist. A racing bicycle should not be purchased 'off the shelf'; it should ideally be made and fitted to the rider: a frame need only be one centimetre too large or too small to have an effect on your style. However, it is not only the size of the frame that is important, there are other properties that you should bear in mind: the frame should be rigid and stiff, but also as light as possible, strong and well made. The power of the cyclist should not be wasted on propelling the unnecessary additional weight of a heavy bicycle.

Tractive, torsional and other stresses, which may add up to several times the rider's body-weight, are produced whilst the racing cycle is being ridden. Forces of up to one and a half times the cyclist's body-weight are produced on the saddle, of one and three-quarters the body-weight on the pedals and as much as twice the body-weight on the handlebars. With all these pressures the weight of a racing bicycle should not exceed nine to eleven kilograms. It has been found that every extra kilogram added to this weight means that a cyclist has to produce one to two per cent more energy at a speed of 35–42kph. This percentage is even higher when climbing or when riding at a higher speed.

A lighter racing bicycle, in which the frame is too 'soft' and 'twisty' does not, apart from the weight, have any advantages, as much of the valuable power you generate can be lost because of these factors. It is therefore most important to select the material for a frame very carefully. All the other components, such as gears, brakes, handlebars, saddle and so forth should also be of equal quality. These are usually so durable that they outlast, or at least equal, the life of the frame (it is not unusual for racing cyclists to use these

Modern time-trialling machine with special handlebars, smaller front wheel discs and short rear triangle.

components for about fifteen years, whereas the frame may need to be replaced after between two and ten years, depending on usage).

Racing cycles are often used for special purposes, such as time trials. When cycling for time trials the rider is completely on his own, racing only against the clock. For this discipline, certain features of aerodynamics are most important since air resistance increases with speed and is in direct relationship to the amount of air turbulence that the bicycle and the rider create.

Wind-tunnel research has brought about the design of new shapes and forms for the bicycle, just as it has for the car; low profile oval tubes for the frame, repositioning of the front brakes behind the top of the forks, repositioning of the brake and gear-levers, narrowing of the rims and tyres and disc-like covers for the wheels. The same research has shown, however, that the benefit of these features is minimal, and so is relevant only for top-class racing cyclists. To all other cyclists, time-trialling machines of this kind are only of psychological advantage since they will probably feel that they are better equipped than any of their competitors.

There are occasions, however, when a racing cycle of this type can actually be disadvantageous. The narrow, oval tubing of the frame may start to vibrate because of the forceful pedalling during a time trial, and the wind can blow straight onto the wheel discs, so causing an awkward ride – this is why riders do without these disc-like covers (particularly on the front wheel) when there is a sidewind blowing. Special time-trialling machines are therefore not suitable for 'hobby' racing cyclists, partly because such competitors cannot get away with a poor performance and need to do as well as possible in every race.

Low handlebars, narrow, high-pressure tyres, a bottle-holder and bottle, a spare tyre and air pump are all sensible accessories, but the aerodynamic style of single components such as brakes, cranks, gears and gear-levers is not especially beneficial, and under British Cycling Federation rules, bicycles fitted with the 'low-profile' style of handlebars are only to be used (because they can cause instability) on special time-trial machines during time trials on road or track.

Equipment

Bicycle Components

The Frame

A bicycle frame is made up of the following components: top tube; seat tube; down tube; head tube; bottom bracket with chainstays and seatstays; rear and front fork ends. The front forks of a cycle do not necessarily form part of the frame, but they are usually mentioned in connection with it. The frame of most cycles is made from tubes that are of the same thickness all over. This means that it is strong, but not very flexible – and, of course, heavy. A heavy-framed cycle is stiff, and tends to absorb both the side-to-side movement of the rider and the bumps from uneven surfaces.

The more specialised the cycle is, the higher the quality of the frame tubes. The signs of a good-quality frame are as follows:

1. The stiffness of a frame determines how much the frame will flex under loading; the shorter and thicker the tubes are, the stiffer the frame is. Hence smaller frames are stiffer than larger frames.
2. The density of the frame material determines its maximum capacity against deformation and breakages. The thickness of the tubes and the quality of the frame material also help determine this. The crucial stiffness and density of the frame demand an opti-

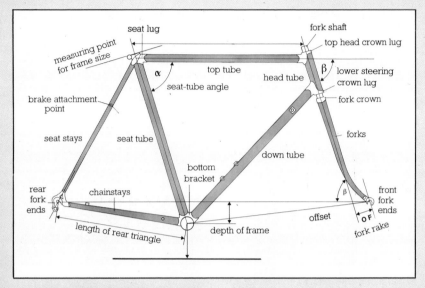

Parts of the frame.

Down tube, seat tube and rear triangle meet in the bottom bracket.

Increased stiffness of the frame is gained through a shorter rear triangle and a curved seat tube.

The tubes of the frame are assembled with lugs.

mal compromise between the choice of material and its thickness.

An alloy of chromium and molybdenum is usually used for high-quality frames, but aluminium, titanium and carbon fibre frames are also available. The ends of the tubes are strengthened as they are subjected to great stress arising from tractive and torsional loads, whereas the middle of the tubes can be made thinner. This strengthening of the ends of the tubes can be found in the well-known Reynolds and Columbus makes. These have seat and top tubes either of 0.6mm thickness in the middle and of 0.9mm thickness at the tube ends or 0.7mm in the middle and 1.0mm at the ends, depending upon the actual type of material used. Further possibilities of improving the stiffness and density of a frame without increasing its weight have been realised in the Columbus SLX-type tubes, in which the seat and down tubes have been strengthened by five grooves (similar to rifling).

Light frames made of good-quality tubes can cushion continual pressure and absorb the shock of a fall or knock more easily. Much more force is needed to damage a frame permanently such as this than a seemingly strong, solid frame of poorer quality; the weight of a frame is determined by its size and by the material from which it is made. A frame made of an alloy of chromium and molybdenum measuring 58cm will generally weigh about 2.5kg, an aluminium frame of the same size about 2.1kg–2.2kg and a carbon fibre frame about 1.6kg–1.8kg.

The importance of the stiffness and of the density of the frame increases with its size. So larger cyclists need a stiffer and heavier frame to prevent it flexing and twisting when riding downhill.

3. The frame geometry is determined by its purpose and by its stiffness. The shorter the frame and the steeper the head-tube angle, the stiffer – and more manoeuvrable – the frame will be. Cyclists with long thighs may sometimes have problems if the head-tube angle is too steep (73 or 74 degrees) – the head tube may be almost parallel with the seat tube, because such cyclists are unable to set the saddle sufficiently far back on the seat pin.

It is generally agreed that for a road-racing bicycle, a head-tube angle of 72.5 degrees with a front-fork trail measuring 40mm results in better handling capabilities, particularly on fast downhill stretches, than the usual frame with a head-tube angle of about 74 degrees and a front-fork trail measuring 50–60mm.

A long frame with head-tube angles of about 70 degrees and a wheelbase measuring more than 100cm absorbs the unevenness of the road surface better than usual frames. Bicycles with this type of frame are suitable for long-distance cycling and touring, and for cross-country or off-road use.

The Made-To-Measure Frame

The measurements of the body should fit the bicycle exactly as this is the only way to develop fully the cyclist's power. Barely two people in the world are exactly the same. Various parts of the body differ from one person to the next – even if two people are of the

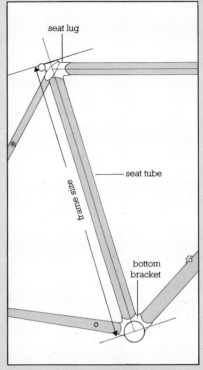

Frame size: the measurement is made along the seat tube and is the distance between the centre of the bottom bracket and the upper edge of the seat cluster (the centre of the top tube).

same height and weight, one might have longer legs and the other a longer torso. However, even if their legs happen to be of the same length, it is possible that one will have longer thighs and the other longer shins.

The length of the arms may also differ from person to person. Because of the great variation between individuals the bicycle should ideally be tailor-made for each rider and the following criteria should be met: the rider should be able to sit comfortably, so that he can transmit power directly to the pedals, and subsequently to the road without wasting energy; the thorax and diaphragm should be able to work freely; and racing cyclists should be able to adopt a more or less aerodynamic position on the bicycle without impairing their breathing or movement.

A bicycle which does not fit the build of its rider can impair the full development of the cyclist's abilities and may also cause physical complaints such as backache, muscle tension and the overloading of joints, tendons and ligaments.

Every frame builder has his own method of determining the perfect frame dimensions and solemnly keeps his formula a secret. However, the most important points for the manufac-

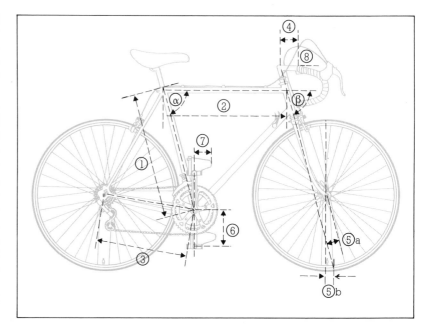

Measurements on the bicycle:
1 frame size, 2 length of top tube, 3 length of rear triangle, 4 length of stem, 5a front fork rake, 5b front fork offset, 6 length of cranks, 7 length of toe-clips, 8 width of handlebars, α seat-tube angle, β head-tube angle.

ture of a quality frame can be summarised as follows. You can quite easily determine the best height for a frame from the height of the cyclist (charts outlining the preferred size for various heights are produced). It is far better, though, to choose a frame slightly smaller than would normally be recommended (because of its inherent stiffness) and to use a longer handlebar stem. For children and teenagers, however, it is better to choose a frame that is the next size up, so that they do not outgrow the bicycle too soon. To determine the recommended size of frame, take the inside-leg measurement (with the rider dressed in cycling

shorts and with bare feet). Multiply this measurement by 0.66 and the result will be close to the correct frame size.

The longer the cyclist's thighs, the shallower the angle between the top and seat tubes ought to be – more like 71 degrees than the usual 75 degrees. The head-tube angle is usually about 73 or 74 degrees, but many cyclists tend to prefer head-tube angles of 72.5 degrees, with a front-fork trail of about 40mm. Some even prefer an angle of 70 degrees for long distance cycling. After having decided the size and the geometry of the frame the builder then calculates the length of the handlebar stem (*see* pages 26 and 65).

It is perhaps advisable to note down all the important measurements and details of your made-to-measure frame in case your bicycle is lost, stolen or damaged – so that a replacement can be constructed to the same specifications without delay.

The determination of inside-leg measurement (bare-foot).

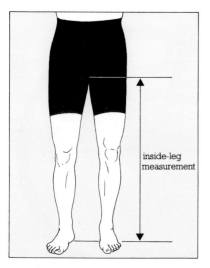

inside-leg measurement

Relationship between size of frame and height of cyclist

height (cm)	frame size (cm)
160–165	51–53
165–170	53–55
170–175	55–57
175–182	57–59
182–187	59–61
187–192	61–63

Equipment

The Steering System

Handlebars and Stem

The handlebars and longer-type stem, usually only found on sports or racing cycles, form a single unit. There are many different types of handlears, ranging from touring handlebars to raised handlebars and to the more common straight design. The wide design of the mountain bike's handlebars are particularly noticeable and aid the handling of the bicycle in difficult terrain.

The larger leverage through these handlebars improves the input of power. However, the more a bicycle is used for sports purposes, the more sense it makes to choose racing handlebars. The curves of this type of handlebar offer many advantages, mainly because there are so many different positions in which to grip these bars.

There are different styles of racing handlebars, two of which are particularly popular. One, the 'Gimondi' type, has soft, round curves with a shorter section in the middle. The other popular design, the 'Merckx' type, also known as the 'straight' racing bar, has a longer middle section. The latter has ample room to grip the top of the bars – the normal touring position. You could say that Gimondi bars are more suitable for racing cyclists who prefer the low-handlebar position, whereas

Top: round, curved style of handlebars with a shorter, straight part in the centre (the 'Gimondi' type).
Bottom: 'even' handlebars with a longer, straight part in the centre (the 'Merckx' type).

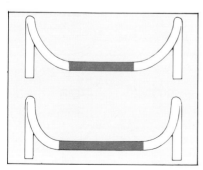

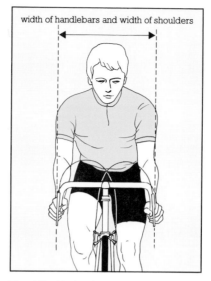

The width of the handlebars should correspond to the width of the shoulders.

The relationship between the size of the frame, the width of the handlebars and the type of cyclist.

type of cyclist	frame size (cm)	width of handlebars
child, youth	up to 51	36–38
small cyclists	51–55	38–39
average height	56–58	39–40
very tall cyclists	59 upwards	40–43

the Merckx type of bars are more suited to those riders who prefer the top position on the bars.

The tubes of the handlebars are usually made from Duralumin about 1.0mm thick and with an outer diameter of 23–25mm. They usually weigh around 350g, while the super-lightweight models weigh perhaps only 250g.

The width of the handlebars is sometimes measured from the middle of the outer curves (centre to centre) or, alternatively, they can be measured from one outside curve to the opposite outside curve (maximum width). These measurements depend upon the type

and manufacturer of the handlebars. Ideally, the width of the handlebars should match that of the rider's shoulders. If the bars are too narrow the cyclist's breathing may be impaired, but if the bars are too wide the arm muscles will quickly tire.

A cyclist of average build will usually require handlebars 40cm wide, whereas smaller, thinner cyclists will need correspondingly narrower handlebars. The ends of the handlebars should always be fitted with end-plugs in order to prevent injuries. (End-plugs are in fact so important that their use forms part of the international rules for competition cycling.) The curves are usually bound with a tape to improve the grip on the handlebars. This tape should become neither slippery in wet weather nor sticky in hotter weather. Accordingly tape made of linen, cotton or cork is particularly recommended. You can also purchase leather coverings, which can be pulled over the bars and then sewn with a strong thread. However, leather coverings lose their grip in wet weather and require the use of racing mitts to improve their grip. Alternatively, you can use a handlebar tape made from plastic or PVC.

How Long Should The Handlebar Stem Be?

The material used for the handlebars, Duralumin, does not rust. However, it does oxidise, especially when body

Racing handlebars with brake-levers and hoods

Equipment

The relationship between the length of the stem and the size of the frame

length of stem (cm)	size of frame (cm)
8–9	51–53
9–10	53–55
10–11	55–57
11–12	57–59
12–13	59–60

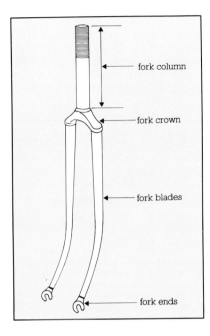

Fork with fork column.

salts find their way to the bars via sweat – and so the handlebars should always be examined for corrosion marks and pitting when you change the bar tape (they are particularly vulnerable around the brake-lever area). The handlebar stem, also usually made of Duralumin, comes in differing lengths – anything from six to thirteen centimetres. The length of the individual stem should be determined by the rider's body measurements. Tables showing fixed relationships between the length of a stem and the size of a frame are available because the rider's body measurements should have already determined the size of the frame.

If you have unusually short or long arms, or perhaps a short torso, this can be accommodated by varying the length of the stem. An accepted ground rule is to choose a frame as short as possible and a stem as long as possible! Because a short frame is stiffer and quite twitchy, a long stem serves, in a way, like 'servo-assisted' steering – essentially it is easier and more comfort-

Handlebars with stem.

able to steer a bicycle with a long stem. The stem is secured into the forks using a wedge bolt.

The Headset

The headset positions and secures the fork column into the head tube while also allowing vibration-free steering. The essential components of a headset are, from top to bottom: locknut; spacer; adjusting race; caged bearings; top head race; bottom head race; caged bearings; fork crown race.

Headsets can be made of steel, Duralumin alloy or titanium, but the cages in which the bearings run are always made of steel. The lifespan of a headset is determined by the material from which it is made and whether or not it has been fitted correctly. It should be fitted in such a way that there is no friction between the handlebars and the forks – so that they turn effortlessly. You should test this when purchasing a bicycle as the proper fitting of a headset is the hallmark of good quality. Premature damage to the cage, the caged bearings and the top head races may

occur if the headset has been fitted either too tightly or too loosely. Consequently the correct fitting of a headset is very important and should be carried out by a craftsman as it is a question of both precision and experience.

The Forks

It can be argued that the forks are actually part of the frame, and indeed they are normally of the same colour, although it is possible to obtain chrome-coloured forks. So far as their function is concerned, the forks belong to the steering system and consist of: the fork column; fork crown; fork blades; and fork ends. The fork column is the part of a bicycle which is subjected to the most strain and is connected to the head tube via the headset. The fork crown must be manufactured very precisely indeed to ensure that it fits exactly into the bottom cone-race of

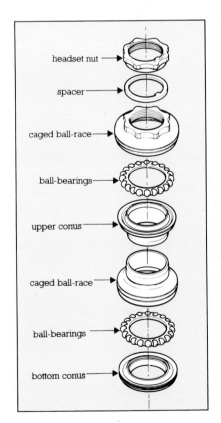

the headset. If this is not the case, the life-span of headset will be shortened.

Forks are of an even thickness all over. They are oval shaped at the top (roughly 28mm at their widest, 19mm at their narrowest) and become almost round towards the bottom (about 12mm in diameter) where they develop into fork ends. The fork follows the same line as the head tube, and is slightly bent forward at the bottom. These two factors determine the way in which a bicycle will respond to steering and riding. Some years ago, when roads were of a poor quality, the curve at the bottom of a pair of forks used to extend for about 8cm. This curve now measures only 3–4cm – sufficient because roads have improved. This shorter curve results in easier steering, smoother braking and less discomfort during high speeds.

Another factor to be borne in mind is the fork rake which is the distance between the extension of the angle of the head tube down to the ground and a perpendicular line from the fork ends to the ground. This measures between 50 and 60mm on a modern racing bicycle (if the angle between the head tube and the top tube measures 74 degrees). Some specialists consider a fork rake of 40mm (with an angle of 72.5 degrees between the head and the top tube) to be more beneficial, particularly when the racing bicycle is predominantly ridden on hilly ground with high-speed descents. Once again

Fork crown with fork and rim brakes.

this shows how much technological consideration goes into the construction of a bicycle.

The Propelling System

When cycling the force is transmitted from the instep of the foot through the shoes on to the pedals and pedal axle. The power continues over the crank and the bottom bracket, which in turn transmits it over the chainwheel on to the freewheel and then to the rear wheel by way of the chain. The power 'continues its journey' over the hub, spokes, rims and tyres of the back wheel, and results in the forward movement of the bicycle. The quality and efficiency of the propelling system is very important, since a large amount of power can be lost during this remarkably intricate process.

The Pedals

Despite the fact that pedals have existed on bicycles for over 120 years real progress has only been made recently. Indeed cyclists do not usually take enough care of these very important components and they are often neglected, resulting in perhaps almost sixty per cent of all touring bicycles having pedals which are too loose, that shake and are damaged by sand, rust or water.

The pedal axle is conical and usually made of a steel alloy. The internal cone of pedals found on modern racing bicycles is positioned directly on the axle which is made in part from titanium, so making the bicycle lighter and shifting the rotation radius towards the inside (the second cone is screwed on to the end of the axle). The axle on racing-bicycle pedals does not go right across the pedal, so enabling the cyclist to lean further to one side or the other when turning corners. Additionally, modern pedals are protected against water, sand and dirt.

Many different types of pedals are

Chainwheels, crank and pedal of a racing bicycle.

available, varying according to the different type of bicycle you own (touring bicycles, mountain bikes and racing bicycles, for example). Racing pedals need to be fixed to the feet.

Toe-Clips

Toe-clips stop the feet slipping off the pedals and also aid the lifting of the pedals so that the result is a smooth, circular movement. The length of the toe-clips depends upon the cyclist's shoe size. When the foot is in its correct position (the instep is positioned exactly above the axle of the pedal) there should be 1–2mm room between the tip of the shoe and the tip of the toe-clips. You can also wind handlebar tape around the toe-clips so that the racing shoes fit better (and are protected from damage).

Equipment

shoe size	type of toe-clip	depth of toe-clips (cm)
37 38 39	short toe-clips	7.5
40 41 42	medium toe-clips	8.5
43 44 45 46	long toe-clips	9.5

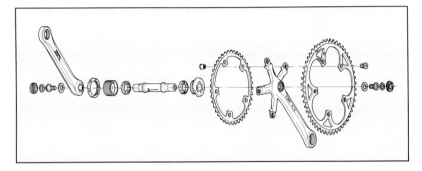

Bottom bracket with crank and chainwheels.

Toe-Straps

Pedal, toe-clip and toe-strap all form a single unit. The toe-strap is 38cm long on average and 1cm wide. It is fastened with safety buckles, which should be positioned at the side of the pedal, so that they do not press on to the foot. The safety buckle should work in such a way that a strap which has been tightened cannot accidentally work loose. It should, however, be possible to undo the strap with one simple movement of the fingers. The tightness of the strap will vary from a loose strap for cycling around town to a very tight strap for hill climbs and sprints.

New Pedal Systems

For a long time there seemed to be no reason for changing the classical system of toe-clips and toe-straps because it worked so well. However, a new idea which is similar to the bindings on a pair of skis has found its way into the cycle trade. An example of this is the 'Look' system, in which toe-clips and toe-straps have become superfluous. Light pressure of the shoe upon the pedal fastens the one to the other, and a light outward twist of the foot releases it instantly. Racing-shoe manufacturers have reacted to this new idea by designing new racing shoes with holes for fastening onto the shoe plates which are needed for this new pedal system.

The Bottom Bracket Set

When cycling, a great deal of power is transmitted through the pedals – at least the cyclist's own body-weight, and perhaps as much as 200–350kg during sprinting. Even greater force is transmitted over the bottom bracket set because of the lifting movements of the crank. The bottom bracket set of a touring bicycle is usually made from steel, but on a racing bicycle, because weight is so important, it is usually made from Duralumin or titanium.

The bottom bracket set is fastened, not surprisingly, inside the bottom bracket of the frame with two lockrings. The set, the crank and the chain-wheel all form a single unit and so should fit together and be of the same make. It is very important to protect these parts from moisture, especially the high quality bottom bracket sets of racing machines. A bottom bracket set should be mounted in such a way that no sideways movement is possible.

Cranks

The cranks are fitted to the bottom bracket axle – one on each side. The right crank has five arms to which the chainwheel is fastened. The length of the crank is measured from the middle of the bottom bracket axle to the middle of the pedal axle. You might think that, according to the common laws of leverage, the longer the cranks are, the less power is needed to turn them. This is in fact the case – but the circum-

Racing pedal with toe-clips and straps.

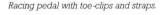

Racing pedal with snap-on mechanism for the racing shoe (the Look system).

ference of the circle which the pedals describe also becomes wider as the crank length increases.

Generation after generation of cyclists have reached the same conclusion so far as the length of the crank is concerned; there is an optimal compromise between the leverage, the transmitted power, the distance the pedals travel for each revolution and the biomechanical lever action of the cyclist's body (in which the length of the thighs is particularly important). The majority of cranks are about 170mm long. Only very large cyclists who need a frame of 60 or 61cm will need a crank length of 172.5–175mm as it becomes more difficult to achieve a high number of pedal revolutions with a longer crank. However, a high number of revolutions is vital during a race in which the speed changes quickly and frequently. Some cyclists prefer a long crank (172.5–175mm) during time trials when the speed is constantly high, the input of power great and the number of pedal revolutions over a given time comparatively low. You will have realised from this how intricate the mechanics – and the biomechanics – of cycling are; just a few millimetres can make a significant difference.

Chainwheels (Chainrings)

A single chainwheel can be fitted to the five arms of the right crank and is quite sufficient for an everyday bicycle. It might be advantageous, however, if you have a need for more frequent changes of gear, to substitute a double chainwheel for a single; these usually comprise a large wheel on the outside (perhaps 52 or 53 teeth) and a smaller one on the inside (normally 42 teeth). Triple chainwheels are also available and are designed for special-purpose bicycles, such as mountain bikes. Chainwheels on a touring bicycle are made from steel and those on racing bicycles from Duralumin.

A chain-guard on an everyday touring bicycle will protect trouser-legs

Aerodynamic cranks and chainwheels.

Asymmetrical, oval chainwheels for overcoming the 'dead centre' more easily.

from oil and from being caught between chain and chainwheel. A chainguard is unnecessary on racing bicycles since competitors usually wear tight clothing. A useful small accessory for a bicycle with a double or triple chainwheel is the chainwheel stud which can save a great deal of trouble as it eliminates the possibility of the chain falling between the outer chainwheel and the crank when changing gear – it is a miserable job to free the chain from this position. This useful little device can also be fitted to the outer chainwheel opposite the crank to prevent the chain slipping off on this side.

Triple chainset for gears in extreme circumstances!

A new development in chainwheels has seen their shape change from circular to oval. The idea behind this new chainwheel is that the optimal direction of power during pedalling always runs perpendicularly to the crank. The impact of this power is at its lowest at the top and bottom 'dead centre'. Accordingly, it seems like a good idea to increase the radius of the chainwheel in these places so that there is a longer lever. Because the impact of power in the horizontal position is greatest, the lever can be shorter here. With the help of computer analysis of pedal movement and pedal power the ultimate chainwheel has been constructed. (The length of the teeth on the chainwheel has also been mathematically designed with particular regard to power capacity.)

When tested during races, however, no improvement was found. This is due to the fact that racing cyclists are used to a higher number of pedal revolutions within a short time and therefore pass the 'dead centre' with power. The ideal 'round pedalling action' also results in an almost perpendicular input of power on to the crank at the top and bottom 'dead centre' through the lifting and lowering action of the toes – so that an oval-shaped chainwheel does not aid the professional racing cyclist.

This is, however, not the case for triathletes, since they are rarely racing-cycle experts and their muscular sys-

Equipment

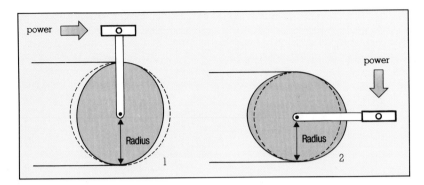

The asymmetrical (oval) chainwheel: 1 increased radius at the upper dead centre of the pedal revolution – resulting in a longer lever. 2 decreased radius in the front horizontal position of the crank – a shorter crank providing a larger input of power.

tem is developed in such a way that they achieve better results when using the oval chainwheel. Indeed many tri-athletes prefer the oval chainwheel because the smaller number of pedal revolutions results in a more efficient biomechanism of the leg movement and more effective power (with less local muscle fatigue). Moreover, the transition in triathlon from cycling to running seems to be made easier by using an oval chainwheel.

Freewheel

The freewheel consists of a body and a number of single cogs of varying sizes, usually made from steel as they need to be very strong. Duralumin or titanium can be used as basic materials or in alloys for lighter freewheel models, but these are much more expensive. These light freewheels are constructed to minimise weight rather than to maximise durability so they wear out more quickly. A freewheel is usually screwed on to the hub. Cassette hubs also exist on to which all the cogs are pushed except the smallest one which is screwed on. The majority of screw-on cogs are built in a similar manner with the two smallest cogs being screwed on and the other cogs being pushed on.

The number of cogs determines whether it is a five-speed, six-speed or seven-speed freewheel. A space of at

A six-speed freewheel of a racing bicycle.

least 4mm must be left between the largest cog and the spokes to ensure that the chain does not touch the near wheel. A spacer positioned here will make sure this does not happen. Six-

speed and seven-speed freewheels can be manufactured so small that they barely take up any more room than the usual five-speed freewheel, but a narrower chain must be used on these compactly-built freewheels because the distance between the cogs is reduced to about 5mm.

Most people choose a freewheel made of steel because it is strong and lasts longer; a six-speed freewheel is usually sufficient and weighs between 360 and 380g. The choice of the individual number of teeth is a science in itself and is often made too complicated. The standard grading in the number of teeth of a six-speed freewheel spanning 13 to 21 is as follows: 13, 14, 15, 17, 19 and 21. If you require a larger cog for hill climbs, the number of teeth might be: 13, 14, 15, 17, 20 and 24. For a five-speed freewheel, the grading in the number of teeth on cogs spanning 14 to 24 teeth could be: 14, 16, 18, 21 and 24. However, cyclists who decide to climb steep mountains and passes need a larger cog than 24 – at least 26 and possibly even 28 teeth (the maximum lies somewhere around 30 to 34). You must remember to test whether the gear body and chain are long enough when using large cogs, like this. It is also important that the grading of teeth has been increased in an exponential and not linear manner so that *useful* gear changes can be made. Generally, fewer cogs of sensible grading offer a larger range of gear changes than a variety of poorly selected cogs.

Freewheel construction.

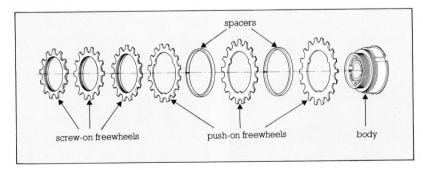

The smallest cogs, having only 13 or even 12 teeth can only be driven round by very fit cyclists, perhaps during time trials or descents. These high gears are, in fact, a disadvantage for most cyclists who are not at their peak of fitness as they stifle the progress towards fitness – and can even destroy a cyclist's good condition. A smooth, round pedal action is much more im-portant for the build-up of the optimal endurance performance.

Speed should be achieved through a high number of pedal revolutions rather than the great power needed to turn a cog with very few teeth. Accordingly, parents should always ask the advice of an expert when buying a bicycle for their children to ensure that they are not putting their muscles under too much pressure.

Equipment

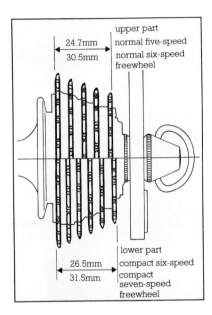

24.7mm — normal five-speed
30.5mm — normal six-speed freewheel

upper part

26.5mm — compact six-speed
31.5mm — compact seven-speed freewheel

lower part

Comparison between normal freewheels and compact freewheels. Six-speed and seven-speed compact freewheels (lower part of illustration) are only slightly wider than the usual five-speed and six-speed freewheels (upper part of illustration).

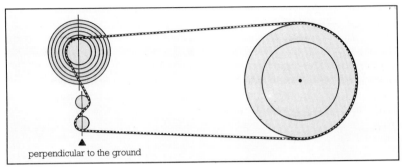

perpendicular to the ground

Chain length: The chain is positioned around the large chainwheel at the front and around the small cog of the freewheel at the back. The length of the chain is correct if the line of the two rolling axles of the gear mechanism runs perpendicularly to the ground in this position.

The Chain

The chain of a touring bicycle either without gears or with hub gears is wider than the chain found on a sports or racing bicycle. The ends of a chain on a touring bicycle are joined with a chain lock, but these are not used on other bicycles as the chain would become stuck in the small wheels or cogs of the freewheel. A chain for a touring bicycle is about 1.4m in length and 7.3–7.8mm in width, consisting of about 108 single links. Every link comprises two rollers each on a pin. These links are joined to each other by both an inner side plate and an outer side plate. A chain weighs between 320 and 390g.

The correct chain length should be determined by a number of different tests. The chain should be tight but not greatly stretched when it is positioned on the large chainwheel (by the pedals) and on a middle-sized cog of the freewheel (at the back of the bicycle). The chain must not sag when running from the smaller chainwheel to the

second smallest cog. The two axles of the wheels (or cogs) of the rear derailleur and the back axle should all be perpendicular to the chain when it runs from the large chainwheel to the smallest cog of the freewheel.

The wear of a chain depends upon two factors; the power applied during pedalling, and rubbing. It is therefore possible to lengthen the lifespan of a chain by oiling and greasing it regularly. The more strain a chain has to take, the shorter its lifespan will be. After a while, a chain becomes longer because the outer side plates stretch from the input of power. This results in

Bicycle chains are so-called 'rolling chains'. Chain-pins connect inner and outer links. Casings allow movement with minimal friction and with only slight wear.

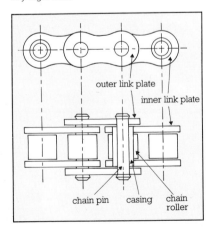

outer link plate

inner link plate

chain pin   casing   chain roller

the distance between the two rollers of each link increasing so that they no longer fit into the spaces between the teeth of the cogs. Moreover, these teeth on the freewheel and on the chainwheel will then become worn and the chain will jump and perhaps even break. You should not let this happen, however, because by this stage a new chain will also require a new freewheel (the new chain will not fit around the worn teeth of the old freewheel). In the long run, it is cheaper to replace the old chain in good time, rather than wait so long that both a new chain and a new freewheel are needed.

You can identify a stretched chain by doing the following test: place the chain around the large chainwheel and then try to pull it away from the teeth with two fingers. If you can pull the chain away from the chainwheel so that the teeth are showing (2–3mm) it is time to replace the old, stretched chain. This usually happens after 1000–3000km depending upon the strain and demand on the chain.

A chain which does not run evenly causes friction and so results in a waste of energy. The ideal chain line runs parallel to the middle of the frame, around the middle of the front chainwheel and around the middle of the freewheel. You can test the chain line of your own bicycle, if you suspect it to be out of line, with the help of a piece of string. The (ideal) line follows the space between the third and fourth cog on a six-speed freewheel. Deviations can be corrected by inserting a spacer between the freewheel and the hub. The chain line is more important while cycling, however. Although it is true to say that you have ten or twelve gears if your bicycle is equipped with a double chainwheel and five or six cogs on the freewheel, it is only theoretically true because the two largest cogs of a six-speed freewheel should only be used with the small chainwheel and the two smallest cogs should only be used with the large chainwheel. The remaining cogs may be used with either chainwheel. If this rule is not followed the chain line will be so uneven that power is lost through the sideways friction of the chain links. This loss of power through friction is not quite so great with the new types of gear and flywheel – but it still exists.

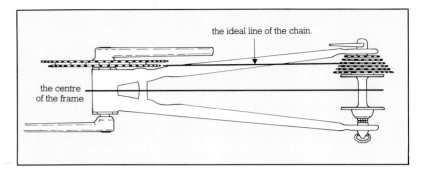

the ideal line of the chain.

the centre of the frame

The ideal line of a chain runs parallel to the frame.

Gears

Gears are necessary if the physical ability of the body is to cope with varying terrain. Having several gears makes it easier to ride an everyday bicycle, for which three or four gears are usually enough. Novice cyclists should perhaps choose an everyday bicycle with hub gears. With this mechanism, the gears have been built into the hub which has a wider diameter than the normal hub.

The usual derailleur gears offer more variety for competitive cycling. The rear derailleur moves the chain from one cog to another by means of a movable lever. A good derailleur should always be efficient, so it is important to look for top quality when purchasing one. It is usually made of aluminium alloys, or in special cases of titanium.

The difference in weight from one derailleur to another is minimal: they weigh around 180–220g, depending upon the make. The chain runs over two wheels (known as the jockey wheels) of the derailleur and is kept taut by them. The top jockey wheel ensures that the direction of the chain is precise – so the derailleur should not show any signs of sideways movement. This wheel should be serviced after every 4,000km cycling (by which time it will have made 2.5 million turns). The derailleur is opened and the rollers and wheels well greased. The top wheel should also be replaced if it moves sideways more than 2mm to ensure that the gear change still works precisely.

The lower jockey wheel, however, should be able to move from side to side so that it can 'stretch' to reach the chain. The derailleur can be adjusted precisely to the largest and smallest cog by using two screws. Most sports, touring and racing bicycles have double chainwheels which increase the number of possible gear changes. The chain is moved from one chainwheel to the other by use of the front derailleur. This derailleur is able to move a chain from one chainwheel to another with a difference of up to twelve teeth. The usual numbers of teeth (either 52 and 42 or 53 and 42) lie well within this region.

Other parts of the gear mechanism are the gear-cables and the gear-levers. Gear-levers are usually positioned on the handlebars of touring bicycles and sports bicycles, but towards the top of the down tube on racing bicycles. A further possibility is to position the gear-levers at the end of the handlebars (instead of plugs).

Cross-country cyclists in particular prefer this position and sprinters also favour it during road-racing because

Efficient and inefficient lines of the chain when changing gear.

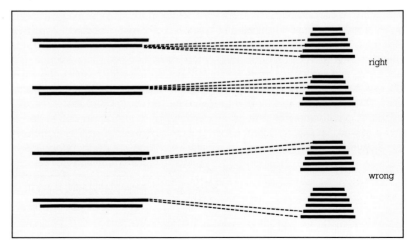

right

wrong

Equipment

The front derailleur.

Gear levers attached to the down tube.

A modern, aerodynamic rear mechanism.

they are able – even when sprinting – to change gear without letting go of the handlebars. Changing gear should be carried out with sensitivity; the pedalling should be relaxed, the force on the pedals should ease off and the levers should be moved just far enough for the chain to fit into the desired gear by carefully listening and feeling for its position. Minor adjustments are often necessary, which experienced cyclists carry out automatically. These subsequent adjustments frequently mean that less experienced cyclists (as well as triathletes) often lose their concentration and some momentum.

For this reason index systems have been developed which make subsequent adjustments unnecessary. A precondition for the correct functioning of these gears is that the top jockey wheel of the derailleur must be constructed in such a way that it does not move from side to side so that the chain always enters the derailleur in the correct position. A great variety of index systems is now available from a number of manufacturers.

Wheels

A wheel consists of a rim, spokes, a hub and a tyre. A wheel should turn easily and, of course, be completely circular. It should not wobble either from side to side or up and down. All spokes should be equally trued – an art which is best left to professionals. Spokes which are too tight are subjected to too much strain during cycling and break easily. The nipples of newly spoked and centred wheels need a settling in period – a distance of around 100km is advisable. The spokes should subsequently be recentred and retightened (this is why new wheels should not be used in cycle races).

Wheels are usually made using 36 spokes. You can also find 32- and 28-hole rims, but these should only be fitted on special occasions such as time trials – not in order to make the wheel lighter, but to decrease the air rotating around the spokes and so decrease air resistance. If the power has to be distributed between a smaller number of spokes, each spoke therefore has to tolerate more strain and so the possibility of broken spokes is increased. A wheel rim with 28 or 32 spoke-holes can twist or buckle if just one spoke breaks so that it is barely possible to continue a race. The advantage of a lit-

tle less air resistance can be lost very quickly and become something of a disadvantage. Sports bicycles and racing bicycles which are used frequently almost always have 36-spoke wheels.

Rims

Rims are made from Duralumin or titanium and must be stiff and strong. The stiffness does not depend so much upon the material but on the geometric accuracy with which the rim is made (that is its width, height and thickness). The lightest rim available is the Nisi Special rim, which is only 19mm wide and weighs around 200g. Lightness, however, is not wholly advantageous since lightweight rims are not indefinitely durable. Cyclists weighing up to 70kg should be riding on rims weighing 300g, and cyclists weighing more than 80kg should be riding on rims weighing around 400g. These rims will have a width of between 20 and 22mm. It is also important to make sure that the sides of the rim are wide enough for the brake-blocks – steel rims, it should be remembered, have a noticeably longer braking distance than aluminium rims.

The shape of a cross-section of a rim depends upon whether it is going to be used with a high-pressure tyre or a tubular tyre. Touring and sports bicycles almost always have high-pressure tyres which need lips at the sides of the rim to hold the tread of the tyre in place. Racing cyclists used only to fit tubular tyres but now it is possible to purchase '700C' high-pressure tyres so narrow that they are considered to be the equal of tubular tyres – particularly for training sessions. Sports rims for narrow, high-pressure tyres are also 20–22mm wide.

The spoke-holes in the rims are under great strain. Little washers or discs measuring 10mm in diameter are worked into the spoke-holes between the nipples and the rim in order to strengthen these against the tractive strain. The spoke-holes are also tilted five degrees in the direction of the spokes in order to relieve the strain on the nipple and spoke thread.

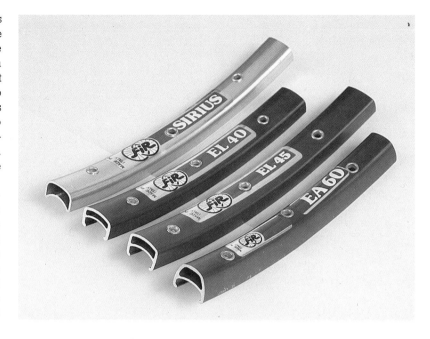

Different types of rim – for tubular tyres (top) and for touring tyres (the other three rims).

Cross-section of a rim for use with touring tyres.

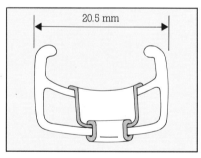

Cross-section of rim for use with tubular tyres.

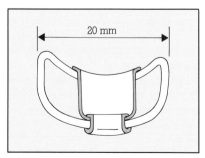

Each illustration shows a cross-section through the middle of the washer of each spoke-hole, which point alternately to the right and left.

Hubs

The hub is the core around which the wheel turns. There are different types of hub, depending upon the type of bicycle. All hubs roll on ball-races, which are to be found between the cup and the cone of the hub. The cone must neither be too tight nor too loose as this will cause the wheel either to turn jerkily or to wobble. A precondition of the smooth running of a wheel is that the ball-races are well greased and free of dirt. The outer discs of the hub are usually positioned about 0.5mm from the cone so the grease of the ball-race must cover the rest of this space. Such protection usually lasts about one year – after this period the hub needs to be taken apart, cleaned and greased.

The edge of the hub, which picks up the spokes, is called the flange. There are two types of flange hubs; small and large (most hubs are small). A wheel made with a large flange hub is harder and stronger because the spokes are shorter than on wheels with small flange hubs. Large flange hubs are usually preferable on wheels with thirty-two spokes or less – or when stronger wheels are necessary for hill-climbing or track cycling. The spoke-holes should be pushed down into the rim, so that the spokes do not break.

A small flange hub for the rear wheel.

Equipment

Nuts, Wing-nuts and Quick-Release Devices

The wheels of touring bicycles (and sometimes sports bicycles) are screwed to the frame with nuts or wingnuts. Wheels of better quality sports bicycles and racing bicycles, however, are all equipped with a quick-release device which allows a wheel to be changed quickly and effortlessly. Every bicycle can in fact be equipped with this gadget; a hollow hub axle is needed so that the axle of the quick-release device can be accommodated. A wheel with a quick-release device can be removed and replaced at the touch of a lever. This is practical and saves both time and tools.

Spokes

A wheel needs to be both light and strong so that it can endure a force of several hundred kilograms – which can arise during cycling. The weakest

A large flange hub with a quick-release device.

A small flange hub with spokes fitted radially.

points in the system are the spokes, which are affected by the following loads:

1. Radial loads. These are in the direction of the spokes and are caused by general pull and pressure, by the cyclist's weight and by the surface of the road (pot-holes or similar).
2. Lateral loads. These are caused by leaning the bicycle to the sides, for instance during 'honking' (standing up on the machine when riding uphill).
3. Torsional loads. These act on the back wheel through the propelling action, the pedal power (transmitted over the chain, freewheel and hub) and then transmitted over the spokes during the forward movement.

The greatest load acting on the spokes occurs where they are bent near the flange of the hub. The second largest load occurs at the end of the spokes near the rim. This is why the so-called 'butted' spokes have been reinforced at the ends (they have a diameter of 2mm at the ends and only 1.6mm elsewhere). Spokes on racing bicycles usually have a diameter of 1.8mm or 2mm and are made from either stainless steel or plated with a layer of chrome.

Spokes are crossed three or even four times in order to achieve a better distribution of the tension. The more the spokes cross each other, the longer they need to be. This also makes cycling more comfortable as the wheels are more 'springy'.

The power mainly affects the bends of the spokes on the side of the free-

A hub (large flange hub) and quick-release device.

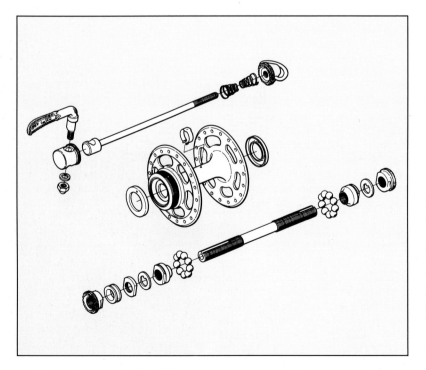

wheel near the hub. This is a danger spot for spoke breakages and is also the area in which it is most difficult to change the spokes because the freewheel must be removed in order to do so. This is why it is particularly important to fit the bends of the spokes properly to the flange. Radial wheels have now been developed in order to avoid the problem of bends in the spokes.

Discs

Disc wheels are in fact normal wheels with spokes covered with a large, thin, light disc – designed to minimise the air resistance which occurs around the spokes. This is why discs of this kind are used in time trials. Surprisingly, these innovations only reduce air resistance by as little as one per cent. This small advantage can easily be lost by side winds – which may even make them disadvantageous. Accordingly, competitors should check the prevailing wind conditions before deciding whether or not to fit discs to their

wheels for a time trial or similar event. A compromise that is generally employed is to use a disc on the rear wheel but not on the front (since it may interfere with the steering).

Tyres

As mentioned earlier, there are two types of tyre; high-pressure tyres and tubular tyres. The usual, everyday bicycle and the majority of sports bicycles are equipped with high-pressure tyres. The high-pressure tyre consists of an exterior tyre, which can be removed, and a tube. The exterior tyre

Nowadays wheels with discs are usually used 'during track racing. Here F. Moser sets the world record for the distance cycled in one hour (in the race at Mexico City, 1984). Note the use of double toe straps because of the high input of power.

Equipment

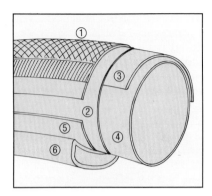

The construction of a tubular tyre: 1 tread (of natural rubber), 2 casing (of cotton or silk), 3 polyurethane belt to protect the inner tube, 4 butly inner tube, 5 base or rim tape, 6 rim.

been developed into thin high-pressure tyres. It is now possible to purchase '700C' high-pressure tyres without wire inserts; the wire has been replaced by other materials such as nylon cord. Such tyres can be folded as though they were tubular tyres and can be carried as spares.

Bicycle tyres should meet the following requirements:

1. They should turn easily.
2. They should not be too heavy.
3. They should be durable.

Accordingly, durable bicycle tyres should have the following signs of quality:

1. Safety: low susceptibility to defects, good road grip.
2. Resistance: low air resistance, low roll resistance, low weight.
3. Comfort: good springiness, easy to repair, easy to reassemble, air and waterproof over a longer period, smooth turn.
4. Cost: reasonable purchase price, long durability, reasonable repair costs.

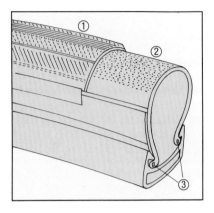

The construction of a touring tyre: 1 tread (of natural rubber), 2 casing (of cotton), 3 lip (with wire or man-made material inlet).

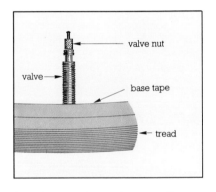

This is the usual valve on tubular tyres. The valve nut has to be unscrewed before the tyre can be inflated.

comprises a rubber casing, a cotton casing and two lips with wire inserts. The tubes of the 'tubular' type have actually been sewn into the tyre. The seam is on the rim side and covered with rim tape and the road side of the tyre is made of a casing formed from the tyre tread.

Tubular tyres are usually narrower and lighter than the common high-pressure tyres and so they are usually found on racing bicycles. The common touring tyres have in the meantime

An assortment of tyres with rims: tubular tyres on the left, touring tyres on the right.

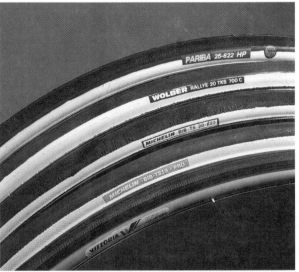

Brake-levers with cables running inside the handlebars.

Modern Modolo rim brakes with short brake-stirrups.

The older type of standard rim brakes by Campagnolo.

Braking System

Each wheel has one brake (this is British law). If one fails to work, a second brake will be available.

Different Types of Brakes

The common bicycle is usually equipped with manually operated brakes on both the front and near wheels in which blocks press against the rim of the wheel. Hub and back-pedal brakes can be fitted to mountain bikes as well as to the common bicycle and the BMX machine. These hub brakes have one distinct advantage; they do not get wet

and so they work effectively – even in the rain.

However, the more sporty a bicycle is and the higher the speed during cycling, the more necessary it becomes to have reliable, effective brakes which do not get too hot during long descents. This is why all racing bicycles are equipped with rim brakes. The braking system consists of brake-levers, brake-cables and the brakes themselves. The brake-levers are positioned on the handlebars in such a way that they can be used equally well from the top and bottom. In the UK the right-hand brake-lever usually activates the front brake and the left-hand lever the rear brake. The levers should not touch

the handlebars – even when pulled as tight as possible. The levers should also move towards the handlebars and not away from them.

The brake cables (made of steel) run through a protective casing and are usually fastened on the outside of the frame. The cables can also be positioned inside the frame for aerodynamic efficiency. This is frequently the case with time-trialling machines. Cyclists who are contemplating undertaking this operation themselves should realise that a hole drilled into the handlebars in the wrong place could affect the stability of the whole bicycle.

There are two different types of rim brake; side-pull and centre-pull

The mountain bike: brake-levers and gear-levers of an 'index' system.

The mountain bike: strong rim brakes with medium pull and long stirrups.

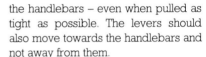

Positioning the brake-cables inside the handlebars of a modern racing bicycle.

Equipment

brakes. It is often difficult to adjust side-pull brakes of poorer quality and so cyclists frequently choose centre-pull brakes for sports bicycles. These brakes hardly ever need readjusting and they work evenly and a little more gently than side-pull brakes. Racing cyclists usually opt for good quality side-pull brakes, however, because they are more effective.

The length of the brake-stirrups is crucial for the efficiency of the brakes; the distance between the axle of the brake and the brake-blocks should be no longer than 7.5cm. Good quality side-pull brakes have a quick-release device at the brake itself or on the levers. You can quickly change the distance between the brake-blocks with the help of this device, perhaps when there is a spoke defect or when the wheel has to be changed for a wider one. The front rim brake on a time-trial machine is sometimes positioned behind the forks for aerodynamic reasons. The brake-blocks are made from a special rubber compound and you must remember to ensure that they are closed at the front – otherwise the rubber could easily be pushed out by the motion of the wheel. The distance between the brake-blocks and the rim should be between 2 and 3mm. The entire block should be in contact with the rim when the brakes are pulled, but they should not touch the tyre.

An elegant racing saddle of excellent craftsmanship.

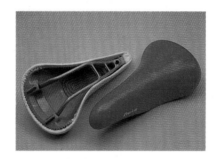

A saddle of strong but light construction.

Saddle and Seat Pin

The saddle has to carry the entire weight of the cyclist – in different positions. The distribution of weight and the area on which the cyclist actually sits change constantly – for example, the cyclist may sit upright or lean forwards. The saddle is one of the most important parts of a bicycle, particularly if you cover long distances. The more upright you sit and the more slowly you cycle (perhaps on an everyday bicycle) the softer and wider your saddle should be. The more competitive you are, however, particularly if you generate a high number of pedal revolutions, the firmer and narrower your saddle should be (in order to prevent your sitting position constantly changing). The upper thighs must not rub the saddle during cycling.

The saddle used for competition may seem to be hard – but it is more comfortable than a soft saddle in the

long run. Real leather saddles are still obtainable but they must be greased and prepared before use (the hardness of these saddles may also be adjusted by means of a screw). The disadvantage of these saddles, however, is that they must be treated after every wet ride to prevent them from losing their shape, and to retain the elasticity of the leather. They are also comparatively heavy at about 600g but some traditional and conservative competitive cyclists still use these leather saddles (such as those made by Brooks). Saddles with man-made casings covered with leather, suede or buffalo leather and stuffed with foam material are often used because they have two great advantages; they require no special care, and are lighter than all-leather saddles, weighing only 300–350g. There are also special saddles for female cyclists which are slightly wider than those for male cyclists. Further choice is available inasmuch as there are now lighter saddles made with an aluminium base weighing only 160–260g, but these are unsuitable for cyclists weighing more than 75kg as they do not provide sufficient support.

The saddle is positioned on a seat pin. Everyday and touring bicycles are frequently equipped with a simple saddle-lock and grid so that the saddle may be easily adjusted. These are useless on racing bicycles as they are neither particularly precise nor very strong and also add extra weight. Seat pins with integrated locks allowing direct adjustment are preferable. Saddles are usually positioned horizontally – indeed it is not a bad idea to use a spirit level. The seat pin should fit the seat tube of the frame exactly, and project into the seat tube for at least 6cm. Seat pins which are too long result in superfluous weight and those which are too short in instability.

Brake-shoes: the brake-shoes of rim brakes must be 'closed' in the direction of cycling!

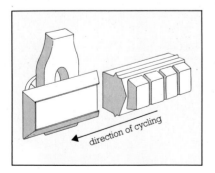

direction of cycling

Time-trialling machines with discs during a two-up time trial (F. Moser and D. Thurau cycling for the Baracchi Trophy in 1986).

Equipment

Special Finishes and 'High Tech'

An exclusive racing bicycle satisfies the desire for perfection and the devotion to detail seems to be instinctive. Indeed some cyclists, for whom cycling is more than a mere physical activity, long to possess a very special, exclusive bicycle. Undoubtedly some get a special feeling when they ride their made-to-measure machine on gloriously sunny days and their eyes meet a well finished, sparkling fork crown, beautiful brakes and a golden, shiny stem – possibly with the inscription of the rider's name on it. The hand touches beautifully finished levers every time the gears are changed and the feet are hooked in bright, golden toe-clips. The friend following behind on another bicycle is impressed by the gleaming, brightly polished stem and lustrous, golden, aerodynamically formed gears. Just about every part of the bicycle, including the frame, can be produced in high-tech style and made of special material. All this, of course, is hardly necessary, but why should everything in life be realistic? Different people enjoy different things. The cyclist who only wants to train and compete needs none of this – but why not?

Accessories

A racing bicycle is really only complete when the most important accessories have been added; spare tyre or tube, tyre-pouch, tools, pump, bottle-cage and bottle. Accessories such as a bicycle computer, mudguards and lights are not absolutely necessary, but can be very useful.

A saddle with pouch.

Spare Tyre, Spare Tube, Tyre-Pouch

Cyclists using tubular tyres should always carry one or two spare tyres with them. It is also sensible to carry a spare tube (or at least a repair kit) when riding on high-pressure tyres. The spare tyre is fastened under the back of the saddle – either by using a toe-strap, or in a tyre-pouch. You can also carry it in a bottle-cage or in a pocket of a cycling top. The spare tyre should always be one that has already been used as it will be much easier than a new tyre to pull up around the wheel rim. It is a good idea to wrap a spare tyre up in waterproof material since it is difficult to keep a wet tyre on the rim.

Pump

It is pointless carrying a spare tyre or tube if you have left the pump at home. Nowadays pumps are usually made of synthetic materials and so are very light. A foot-pump with pressure gauge is also useful, so that the desired pressure for the tyres can be reached exactly before setting out on a cycle ride. It is also easier to use a foot-pump than a hand-pump.

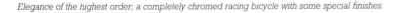
Elegance of the highest order; a completely chromed racing bicycle with some special finishes.

Tools

Cyclists need two sets of tools; one set carried on the bicycle and the other left at home for minor repairs and general maintenance. Useful tools to be carried on the bicycle include tyre-levers, a small screwdriver for a variety of uses such as the adjustment of gears, Allen keys (5mm and 6mm) for all important 'screws', spoke-key and spanner for the most important bolts.

> Hint: it is possible to make a screwdriver by filing the long end of an Allen key, so making it unnecessary to carry a separate screwdriver.

Bottle-cage and Bottle

Bottle-cages made of Duralumin are very light, weighing only about 50g, and are attached to the down tube of the frame. If a second bottle-cage is desired, this may be fixed to the seat tube.

Bottles are made of synthetic material and the 'lid' has been constructed in

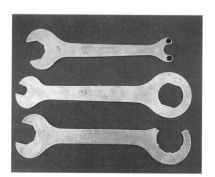

Special spanners for bottom-bracket sets and headsets (depicted on a smaller scale than the tools on the right).

Bottle-cage with bottle (here covered in leather).

such a way that it can be opened with the mouth during riding. A bottle usually has a capacity of 0.5l (it is also possible to obtain larger bottles with a capacity of 0.75l). The air resistance of a round bottle is roughly equivalent to that of a tyre. This is why it makes more sense to use the narrow, aerodynamic bottles during high-speed cycling. You can now purchase a thermos flask with or without a casing which will keep a hot drink warm during the winter and a

cold drink cool during the summer. (It is also possible to buy casings which can be pulled over the bottles.)

The Computer – the Eye of the Coach

There was a time when you had to guess the distance you had cycled, but no longer. Today, there are few simple milometers – which merely count the distance you have travelled – on the market. Technology in the guise of the microchip has offered cyclists milometers which normally fulfil four functions and can be read by pressing a single button; speed, distance covered on that particular day, total number of kilometres (miles) and average speed.

This data should be presented precisely, quickly, easily and legibly. An electronic device (which will often fit into a matchbox) will satisfy these conditions as well as being water- and shatter-proof. A minimal amount of en-

Some very important tools which should always be carried on longer trips.

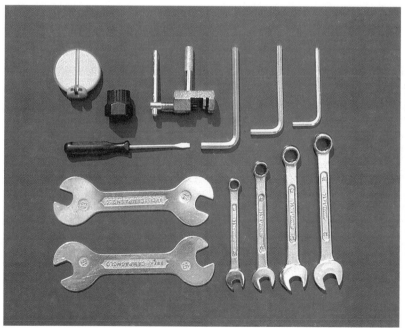

Equipment

A bicycle computer, the Ciclomaster, fitted to the handlebars.

Light plastic mudguards for racing bicycles.

You should regularly test the following on your bicycle for safety reasons; these should be checked before every journey:

1. Are both wheels turning evenly and smoothly?
2. Is the tension of all the spokes more or less the same?
3. Are all the nuts, wing-nuts and quick-release devices tight?
4. Are the tyres in a sound condition – or are there holes or slits in the outer casing? Are there any loose threads?
5. Is the tyre pressure correct?
6. Have the brakes been properly adjusted (brake-blocks parallel with the rim and closed at their front, the brakes engaged with a short action on the levers)?
7. Are the gears properly adjusted, and do they work perfectly (an easy transfer from large to small chainwheel and vice versa; an unhindered movement of the chain at the back of the bicycle on the smallest and largest cog – without touching the spokes or the frame)?

Rear mechanism with adjustable screws.

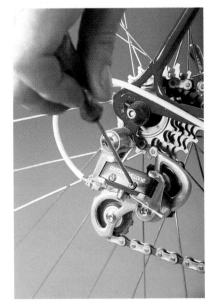

ergy is needed; batteries, which last at least one year, may be required although some computers are equipped with their own solar cells. Some more sophisticated computers offer readings of pedal revolutions per minute and, with an additional device, readings of your pulse.

In this way the computer can guide and keep an eye on the intensity and quantity of your training, rather than a coach independently recording your speed, pedal revolutions and pulse. The idea of a computer is not to encourage the cyclist to ride faster every day but to form a well considered training routine with the necessary regular changes in intensity and quantity.

It is not always advisable to increase your speed from training session to training session, although this happens without the cyclist realising it. The computer helps give the cyclist the information for planning a less intense training schedule. It might also be an idea to record the computer data in a book after training as it can prove to be valuable support for a long-term training schedule. One vital precondition for the accuracy of the computer data is that the size of the wheel must be entered into the computer as exactly as possible.

Mudguards

Most bicycles are equipped with mudguards in order to protect the cyclist from spray and dirt from the road. Racing bicycles do not usually have mudguards but these can be most useful – and desirable – in bad weather (it is not difficult to attach narrow light mudguards to a racing bicycle). You can also buy a mudguard for the rear wheel with a rear light and a light cable running underneath.

Lights

It is sensible to fit lights to a racing bicycle, especially in the autumn when the clocks are put back to winter time. Special light systems incorporating dynamos are perhaps the best idea. The dynamo is fitted under the bottom bracket and rubs against the tyre, the movement of which generates electricity. Front and rear lights can be clamped to the handlebars and to the seat pin respectively. Reflective stripes on your clothing are advisable as they 'throw back' the light from cars' headlights twenty times stronger than that from bicycle lights.

Care, Maintenance and Repair

Cyclists who love their bicycle – and who value their own well being – will care for and maintain their bicycle regularly. They should at least be able to master the basic skills such as changing a tyre, a chain and a freewheel and broadly know how to centre spokes.

Cleaning the Bicycle

The average bicycle is, of course, a means of transport; the mountain bike is solid and the racing bicycle a valuable, precise instrument. Nowadays every bicycle is well made and quite strong in every type of weather. Both the frame and the various accessories (particularly if they are made from Duralumin or titanium) are stainless, but you should nevertheless service your bicycle regularly – as many top racing cyclists do. They service their bicycle after a long, rainy ride before they 'service themselves'. It is, in fact, easy to look after a bicycle. You require the following items: a bucket of water with washing-up liquid; a sponge and brush; a paint brush and container of petrol, some paraffin, some bicycle oil, some bicycle grease and a protective wax spray.

It is best, if the machine has quick-release devices, to remove both wheels from the bicycle. The spokes, hubs and rims should be cleaned with a soft brush and the frame and all other major bicycle components with a sponge and soapy water. The bicycle should shine from the silicone in the detergent without having to be dried off. The bottom bracket, the hubs and the headset are usually well greased, so they do not often need to be further protected against moisture. If the chain is very dirty, it should be cleaned with a small paint brush and petrol, diesel

A bolt with support for the chain – for easier bicycle maintenance.

oil or paraffin before you wash the bicycle. It should then be greased with chain grease and can also be oiled.

The freewheel is likewise oiled after the cycle wash. Place the rear wheel flat on the ground with the freewheel uppermost and put two or three drops of oil in the freewheel body. You should also put one drop of oil on each of the following; the cables of the chain gear, the joints of the front derailleur and the moving parts of the brakes.

You will reap great rewards by servicing your bicycle and its components regularly; defects will become apparent at an earlier stage and you will notice when the brakes do not grip evenly and need correcting, when the gears need adjusting, when the chain needs replacing, when a toe-clip is bent or whatever. Moreover, it gives you a feeling of security if you have

made sure that the bicycle is safe to ride.

The finishing touch is to coat the frame, seat pin and movable components with a protective layer of wax which can be sprayed on from a can.

Important: You should undertake a thorough examination of your bicycle once a year; hubs, bottom brackets and headsets should all be dismantled and greased with bicycle grease. Even a very thick coating of grease does not stop the penetration of water, dirt and grit which can hinder the proper function and so bring about increased wear of the bicycle.

Tyre Care and Tyre Storage

High-pressure tyres are usually less delicate than tubular tyres. High-quality, expensive, tubular tyres which are used for training and sometimes for racing should be stored as though they were mature wine! Brand new tyres have not yet reached their full 'maturity' – and are more susceptible to defects than stored tyres; what happens is that the rubber ripens and hardens and certain components of the rubber evaporate during storage. This is why tubular tyres should be stored for a period of one or two years, preferably on a rim and slightly pumped up (3 to 4 bar) in a cool, half-lit room. The tyres should be sprayed with silicone rubber from time to time during this period to prevent them from drying out, and to keep the tyre exterior supple.

Equipment

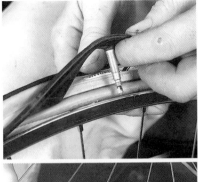

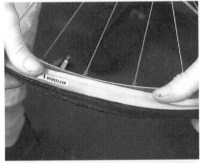

Changing the tube on a touring tyre. First the valve is placed into position, then the tube is inflated slightly and placed under the tyre. Next the tyre is pushed on to the rim by hand, being careful not to damage the tube.

How to Change a Tyre

High-pressure tyres are easily changed with the help of tyre-levers. The most important stages of a tyre change are shown in the sequence of illustrations above. It is particularly important to ensure that the tube is not showing under the lip of the outer tyre because the tube will tear as it is being pumped up.

Tubular tyres have to be glued on to the rim, either with rim cement or with sticky rim-tape. It can prove difficult for novices to pull the tyre up over the rim but it is important to do this properly if the tyre is to be kept safely on the rim during high-speed downhill rides and when turning corners. (*See* the instructions below and the illustrations on the following page.)

The tyre is initially slightly loosened opposite the valve and pulled away from the rim. The tyre can now be removed from around the rim (*see* illustrations 1, 2 and 3). The valve hole can be cut with a triangular scraper so that the lip around the valve does not form a bump (*see* illustration 4). Glueing the rim-tape on is a clean, easy and relatively safe job. The only problem that may arise is that during longer descents while the brakes are on the heat that this generates can reduce the stickiness. This is why professional cyclists prefer tyres that have been fixed with rim cement. Rim cement needs at least twenty-four hours to dry if the tyre is to stick properly. However,

the rim cement will dry out completely after a few months reducing the adhesion of the tyre to the rim so that it is no longer absolutely secure. This is the reason why in races racing cyclists only use wheels with freshly fitted tyres.

Initially a tyre should be pulled up around the rim without using any rim cement or rim-tape so that it is stretched. Three or more layers of rim cement, each with a drying time of about a day, should be applied to the rim. This will create a good, thick layer of ground material (*see* illustration 6). Fitting a tyre on this prepared ground material will take about ten minutes after you have applied another layer of rim cement.

The next step is to pump the tyre up slightly so that it contains a small amount of air. The wheel is now positioned upright with the valve hole at the top; the valve is then placed through the hole in the rim. Now hold the tyre with both hands and push it down around the rim with continued pressure of both thumbs, until all of the tyre has been stuck down around the rim (*see* illustrations 7, 8 and 9). A length of about 5cm of the rim opposite the valve should be left free of rim cement, so that it will be easier to remove a damaged tyre starting from this point. The tyre is then aligned on the rim so that the wheel turns smoothly and evenly. Turning the wheel at an angle, both to the left and to the right, over a distance of about ten metres should secure the tyre to the rim (*see* illustrations 11 and 12).

When changing a tyre with rim-tape, first clean the rim of grease and oil. Then apply the rim-tape all around the rim, starting at the valve hole. Rub the tape with the handle of a screwdriver, a rounded wooden stick or shaft of a hammer so that the tape is properly fixed to the rim and so that the side of the tape which faces the tyre is roughened. Pump the tyre up to about 5 bar after the fitting and align it around the rim so that it turns evenly and smoothly.

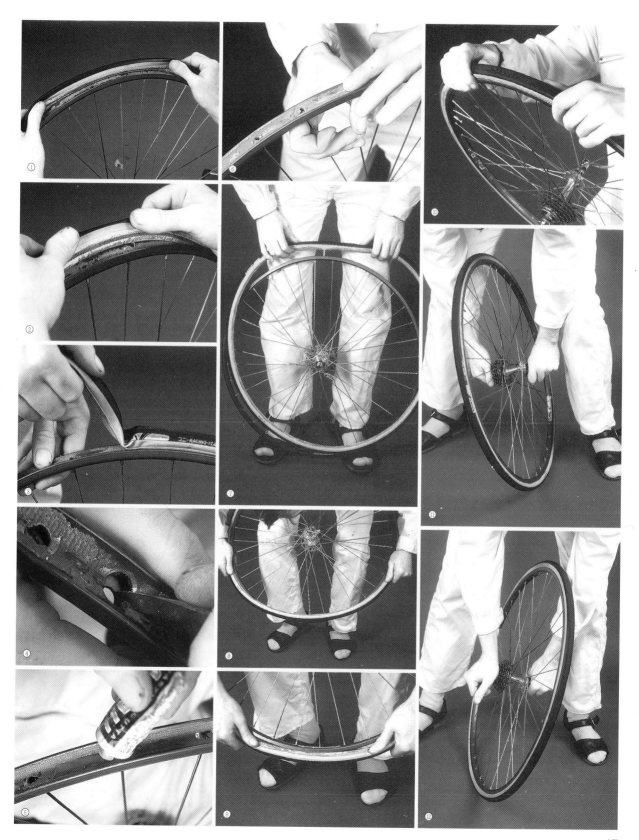

Equipment

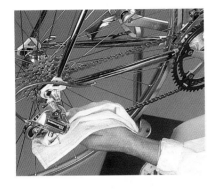

Chain maintenance: use a rag dipped in oil or grease.

Maintenance of the Chain

The chain only works efficiently and with minimum friction when it is clean, grit-free and sufficiently greased or oiled. It should therefore always be cleaned after rainy rides, rides along sandy roads and generally whenever it has become dirty. It is possible to do this with a small paint brush and some petrol or paraffin although special chain gadgets – which are applied around the chain with chain-cleaning fluid – are also obtainable. The chain is moved forward through the wire brushes of this gadget until it is clean.

Once you have done this the chain should be greased with chain grease.

Replacing the Chain

As mentioned earlier, the chain should be replaced regularly. You should not leave this so late that the stretched links of the chain have started to wear out the teeth of the freewheel and chainwheel as this would necessitate the replacement of the freewheel each time the chain is replaced. The longer lifespan of the freewheel easily compensates for the cost of the more frequent replacement of the chain. It is, therefore, well worthwhile mastering the skill of changing a chain.

Shortening the chain in order to make it just the right length is all part of this skill. A screwdriver is sufficient for those bicycles equipped with chain link locks. Bicycles with derailleur gears, however, do not have a chain link lock. To replace a chain you will need either a chain-rivet extractor or chain-rivet pliers. These are used to push out the rivet of one chain link – taking care to leave one end in the loop of the chain (*see* illustrations 1, 2 and 3). The length of the chain can

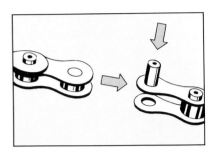

The joining of chain links.

now be adjusted and the chain replaced around the cog and derailleur. The chain is then reconnected by pushing the ends together and putting the pin back in its place, using the chain-rivet extractor or pliers, so that it juts out abut 0.5mm on either side of the chain. Do not forget to test the free movement of this link; blockages can be removed by bending the chain from side to side, until the link moves easily (*see* illustration 6).

An assortment of chains: different chains – of different workmanship.

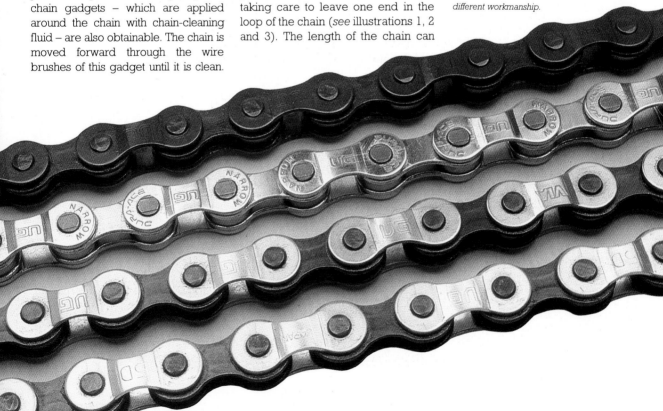

Replacing the Freewheel

The freewheel must be removed if you want to change the gear ratio or if you need to pull a spoke through the hub on the side of the freewheel. The tool needed for this, not surprisingly, is a freewheel remover. These vary in shape and size according to the make of freewheel – some are no larger than a matchbox and weigh only 30–50g so that they can be fitted into a tyre-pouch or the pocket of a cycling top (the freewheel is actually removed with a fitting spanner). The new freewheel can then be easily screwed on by hand without the use of any tools.

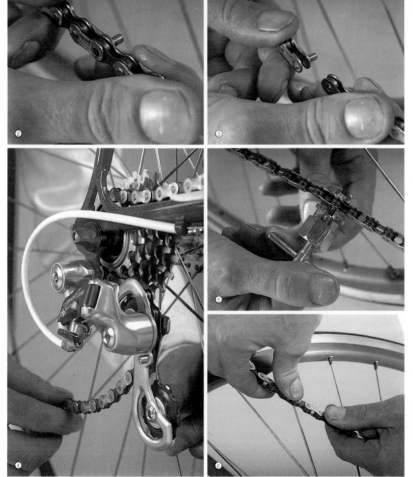

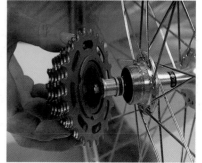

Equipment

Trueing Wheels

The proper, perfect trueing of a wheel is an artform which few experts can master. Independent cyclists should, however, be able to tighten spokes which are noticeably loose and adequately true a wheel with a slant to one side so that you can continue cycling. For this you require nothing more than spoke keys and the ability to realise which way to turn the spoke key either to tighten or loosen the spoke! Trueing must always be done slowly and patiently. If you need to correct a tendency to one side of the wheel or the other, several spokes will need to be corrected. If the rim has a bias towards the left, then the spokes in this area will have to be turned once with the spoke key, initially on the right side of the rim. The spokes on the left side of the rim in the same area will now have to be loosened by turning them once with the spoke key. In other words, the spokes are always trued alternately: tightened on the right and loosened on the left and so on until the wheel turns more or less evenly. You must ensure on finishing, that there are no spokes either too loose or too tight.

Possible adjustments of gears: the two illustrations at the top show the position of the front derailleur; the three lower illustrations show the adjustment screw of the rear mechanism. You should remember that the workmanship is different from one manufacturer to another.

Spokes can be readjusted with a spoke key.

Adjusting Gears

The gear and derailleur mechanism is one of the most reliable and economic systems for transmitting power. It needs comparatively little care – although careful adjustment is vital for its correct function.

The range of movement of the rear mechanism and of the front derailleur is each limited by a set of two screws. One of the screws of the rear mechanism prevents the chain from falling off the largest cog and into the spokes and the other screw prevents the chain falling off the smallest cog and down between the freewheel and the ends of the frame. The front derailleur also has

to be adjusted so that the chain can fall neither to the inside nor the outside of the chainwheels. Select the largest or smallest cog and the small or large chainwheel; then adjust the small screws at the top of the derailleur to ensure the correct range of movement. Finally you should ensure that the chain runs smoothly in all gears without rubbing against the spokes, frame or derailleur. This is simply done by repeatedly changing the gears up and down and that is that – there is nothing more to be adjusted.

Adjusting Brakes

Racing bicycles usually have side-pull brakes which have been attached to the forks and seat stays with Allen screws. The front and rear brakes are initially fastened slightly with an Allen key. The brake-stirrups are then pushed down on to the rim using your hand and the cable is now pulled tight. On releasing the brake-stirrups a distance of about 2mm between the rim and the brake-blocks will usually be left – the correct distance for perfect functioning of the brakes. Final adjustments can be made by turning the screw above the extension of the brake-stirrups.

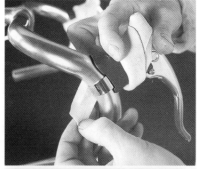
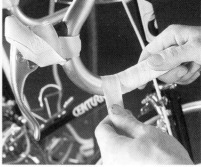
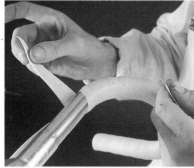

Minor adjustment to the rear stirrups.

Applying Handlebar Tape

The application of handlebar tape starts at the brake-levers. The lever hoods should be lifted slightly and a strip of tape should be applied to the clip of the brakes (the strip of tape should be long enough to reach far enough under the lever hoods). The handlebars are now wound with tape, starting at the ends and working towards the middle, making sure that the tape is applied at equal distances between layers with the same amount of tape overlapping each time. The tape is applied in a figure of eight around the brake-levers. Whether you complete the tape application a little way before the ferrule or continue winding up to it depends upon individual preference and 'grip habits'. The last piece of tape is cut diagonally and fastened with insulating or similar adhesive tape (which is often supplied with the handlebar tape).

Overleaf: the sport of cycling amidst an impressive range of mountains; Fons de Wolf on the Galibier in the Tour de France.

Equipment

Bicycle Transport

There are several sensible reasons for transporting a bicycle on a car. Cyclists living in town, for instance, might want to drive far enough out to reach quiet roads – or a family might want to go on holiday and take their bicycles with them in order to explore new countryside. If you are on your own, it is easy enough to transport a racing bicycle; the wheels can be quickly removed from the frame and all parts can be packed into the boot. However, it is a good idea to purchase a roof-rack as the boot may often be full of luggage and your bicycles' wheels may not

The essentials of a cyclist's wardrobe.

Transporting bicycles on a special roof-rack, a common sight at races.

Attaching the bicycle at the forks and at the rear wheel gives the most stable position for transporting machines.

easily be removed. You could also perhaps use a luggage carrier, depending upon the type of car, or special bicycle carrier designed for caravans.

Bicycle carriers can usually transport three or four bicycles although some can carry more than this. There are in principle two ways of transporting bicycles, the bicycle can be positioned upside-down and fastened at the saddle and handlebars or it can stand upright in which case it will be fastened with a bar (the front wheel is normally removed and the forks attached with a quick-release device). The latter option is the more stable. You can now purchase bicycle roof-racks which can be locked in the same way that roof-racks for skis can be. Most bicycle roof-racks

are versatile and can be used for transporting surf-boards and skis. If necessary, special bags and 'suitcases' for transporting bicycles safely on a flight can now be obtained.

Clothing

Obviously the speeds reached when cycling are faster than when walking or running. This is very comfortable on hot days as the wind generated has a pleasant, cooling effect. You should also remember, however, that the body becomes colder on cold days than it would without that same wind. This is why clothing should be appropriate for both warm and cold days. Serious cyclists need clothing for hot days as well as for cold days.

> Important: bicycles transported on a roof-rack create greater wind resistance than a surf-board or a pair of skis. It is therefore imperative not to drive faster than 120kmh (75mph) when transporting bicycles.

Leggings for changeable weather conditions and temperatures.

The chamois-leather insert in cycle shorts

Overall View and Regulations

The regulations for the clothing worn during competitions organised by the British Cycling Federation (BCF), require all competitors to wear racing shoes, shorts, vest and crash hat.

Cycle clothing should, in principle, protect the following vulnerable parts of the body: the back (kidney area, lumbar vertebrae); buttocks; feet and hands. The kit of a well-equipped cyclist would include the following items of clothing:

1. Cycle shorts (shorts with padding and/or dungarees, leggings).
2. Racing shoes (summer and winter types).
3. Overshoes (rain and thermal types).
4. Socks (short, white socks and v. arm, woolly socks).
5. Cycle tops (long and short-sleeved).
6. Vests (absorbent and 'able to breathe').

7. Gloves (for summer, warm mittens for winter).
8. Head gear (cycle hat, sweat band, cycle helmet and/or cap, woolly hat for winter).
9. Rain clothing (rain jacket, rain leggings, rain overshoes).
10. Thermal suit.
11. Protective glasses.

Cycle Shorts

It is, of course, possible to train without proper cycle shorts, but these can often become the most important piece of clothing a cyclist possesses if he decides to train regularly and for a long period of time. They are made of wool or man-made stretch fabric. The most important feature of a pair of cycle shorts is the insert which is often made of chamois-leather. This insert protects the buttocks during cycling. The legs of the shorts should cover at least one third of the cyclist's thighs, and lie flat against the skin without creasing. The waistband should not cut into the waist. Braces between vest and cycle top ensure that the shorts do not slide down during cycling. The legs are protected either with leggings which are pulled up over the bottoms of the shorts or long racing trousers worn over the shorts.

When cycling you should always take care to avoid saddle-soreness, so you should never sit on a dry leather insert but rather apply some cream specially designed for this purpose, or

Different types of cycle shorts.

Equipment

Modern racing shoes with velcro fastening and shoe-plates.

Racing shoe with the clip-on pedal (Look) system.

Lace-up racing shoes with leather sole and shoe-plates.

at least some Vaseline or a cream containing glycerine. This prevents inflammation as well as the development of septic hair follicles, boils and abscesses. This is an aspect of your health which is very important and should not be ignored.

Racing Shoes

There is no reason why you should not use normal, everyday shoes or trainers for cycling – even on longer journeys. In fact, competitive cyclists sometimes wear trainers during cycle training in winter when it is very cold. However, every cyclist who trains regularly should otherwise use proper racing shoes. Their thick, stiff soles aid the transmission of maximum power on to the pedals. The optimal pressure is transmitted from the instep of the foot. Racing shoes can also aid the smooth and even turning of the pedals (a precondition for an optimal cycling style) with the help of shoe-plates which are attached to the soles of racing shoes. It should be obvious that just a few deviations in your cycling style can have a pronounced effect on performance and cause unnecessary strain on joints, tendons and ligaments when you may perhaps achieve a total of several million pedal revolutions a year. A good pair of racing shoes should, in principle, fulfil the following requirements:

1. They should be narrow but not so much that they press against the foot or restrict circulation.
2. The soles should be stiff and solid to gain optimal power transmission and they should have holes to allow the air to circulate and the rain-water to drain off.
3. They should be light in weight.
4. With the shoe-plates on the soles, the pedals, the toe-clips and the toe-straps, they should form a single unit.

Overshoes for rain and cold weather.

The shoes must be narrow and fit properly so it is usually a good idea to buy them half a size too small as they will gradually widen through continued use and through moisture. If a new pair of racing shoes is too tight, you should – bizarre as it sounds – slip them on and then stand in some lukewarm water. You should follow this by a training ride which will dry the shoes to the ideal shape. Ideally you should only choose top-quality cycling shoes, because they are such a vital part of your kit. Racing shoes are meant to be for cycling and not for walking. Walking in them would result in the soles losing their solidity and in the shoe-plates being worn down. This is why you should not put the shoes on until you are just about to get on your bicycle; similarly you should remove them as soon as you dismount. Racing shoes also need care – particularly when they have become wet and dirty on a rainy ride. Wet cycling shoes should be stuffed with newspaper and dried in the air and not on the radiator which will cause the leather to become brittle and rough. Racing shoes dried in the correct fashion can be thoroughly cleaned. This is done with a soft brush and a good, impregnating leather-shoe polish.

The shoe-plates which are usually of man-made material, are of vital importance. The correct fitting of these shoe-plates is imperative if you are to have good cycling style. A deviation of only one millimetre from the ideal positioning can disturb the entire biomechanism of pedalling. Complete systems with fastening between pedal and racing shoe are also available; one example being the Look pedal system. The shoe snaps into the pedal with one movement of the foot – just as ski boots snap into the bindings of a pair of skis – so making the toe-clip and toe-strap superfluous. No doubt time will tell whether this new system is preferable to the older style of shoe-plates, toe-clips and toe-straps; in the new system the sole of the shoe is only fixed to the pedal at one point, whereas in the older method both the toe and the bridge of the foot are also supported while the pedal is pulled upwards.

Cyclists wear short, white socks; they all do it, as you can see!

Skin sleeves are useful in changeable weather conditions.

Overshoes

Certain weather conditions demand that overshoes be worn over racing shoes in order to protect them. It is therefore advisable to wear rain overshoes in wet weather to protect both shoes and feet from moisture. As feet often grow particularly cold when cycling, you may wish to consider buying a pair of thermal overshoes which, as their name implies, protect the feet from growing too cold – or even from freezing.

Socks

In cycling, white socks are the norm. They should reach up just over the ankles and are usually made of wool or cotton although thick, woolly socks should be worn during very cold winter weather. Some professional cyclists even pull thick socks up over their racing shoes when it is very cold. This is most effective since it is possible to train even during quite low temperatures without having to use special thermal overshoes.

Cycling Tops

Cycling tops are available with short sleeves for summer cycling and long sleeves for winter cycling. Cycling tops are both useful and practical. They protect the body from the cold, quickly draw sweat outwards, and fit closely around the body without fluttering – as well as providing protection for the back, particularly in the area around the kidneys. The cycling top must therefore be long enough to cover the lower part of the back while the cyclist is leaning forward on the bicycle.

Cycling tops used to be made from wool but they now comprise special man-made fibres in a number of layers, which can 'breathe' and are simultaneously wind resistant on the outside and sweat absorbent on the inside. A wide choice of cycling tops in many different colours is available, so why not take advantage of this and – quite literally – add colour to cycling (motorists are also more likely to notice cyclists who wear colourful tops). Cycling tops with advertising

slogans can hardly be avoided today but advertising alcohol and tobacco is forbidden – I believe that no athlete of any discipline should promote these goods.

Skin sleeves are available for rides in changeable weather and for warming up before a race. Similar to leggings, skin sleeves are also useful during touring when you set out early in the morning in the cold but when temperatures are likely to rise later in the day.

Vests

Vests made of a special mixture of man-made fibres that draw the sweat off the body towards the outside are most popular. Indeed you should always wear a vest under a cycling top – even during the summer. It can also be a good idea to carry a spare vest in a cycling-top pocket – perhaps when riding in mountains you reach the summit soaked in sweat and then have to face the long and speedy descent. You

Equipment _____

could easily catch a cold wearing a soaking wet vest so, if time permits, change the vest on the summit.

Racing Mitts

Cyclists should always wear mitts, even during the summer – at least during competitive cycling. Racing mitts which have no fingers can also be called track mitts as track cyclists who have no brakes will sometimes stop their bicycle by gripping the front wheel with these mitts. Another reason for using mitts is that they protect your hands when you ride holding on to the brake levers for a long time. They are also useful for removing small stones or grit from the front wheel during cycling and in an accident will help protect your hands.

There are different kinds of mitts, but most are made of soft leather on the palm with either woollen or man-made material on the backs of the hands. The leather on the palm is layered and acts as a type of cushion both against the shocks of the handlebars and the formation of blisters during long rides. Mitts made only of leather are also available, but this leather must be very durable and able to soak up sweat; peccary leather is particularly suitable. Racing mitts should always be tried on by the cyclist who is going to wear them. They must fit tightly but not cut

Racing mitts of thin material.

The racing cap.

A sweatband of absorbent material.

into the hand or hinder circulation. Mitts which are too large will fall into folds around the hands, can slide out of place and affect the grip on the handlebars. You should use gloves with long fingers (such as ski-gloves) on cold days; for very cold weather special thermal gloves are also available.

A racing crash hat, here worn over a racing cap.

Racing Cap and Sweat Band

Most important of all, sweat should not run into your eyes when cycling. This can be prevented by using either a racing cap with a strip of sweat-absorbent material around the edge or a sweat band. A racing cap also protects the head from the sun, and from excessive heat loss during descents. (Fausto Coppi, the famous racing cyclist, used to protect his head from the heat by placing a cabbage leaf on his head under his racing cap!) You can also choose special woolly hats which also protect the ears from the cold during the winter.

A streamlined racing helmet – only used in track races and time trials.

Crash-helmets

It is a rule in many British cycling associations to wear either a crash-hat or a crash-helmet during races; the latter is the safer of the two. British law does not cover this matter. Crash-hats are made of padded leather strips and fastened under the chin. They only protect the head in places and in an accident the leather strips may be pushed aside. Crash-helmets, however, are manufactured from strong, man-made material and have the extra benefit of being comparatively light. They also usually have small holes to allow the air to circulate underneath. Although they are slightly less comfortable in hot weather than crash-hats, crash-helmets are nevertheless preferable from the point of view of safety – and so cyclists should always consider wearing them. Novices, especially, should follow this ground rule as they are more likely to have an accident than experienced cyclists. Statistics show that cyclists who have had one or more falls are likely to crash again. Although professional cyclists usually avoid wearing protective head gear altogether, this must not be a general rule for the inexperienced cyclist.

Waterproof Jackets and Leggings

Some cyclists train under the motto 'Bad weather does not exist – but bad clothing does' and cycle even in cold, wet weather. Cyclists who dislike rain can, of course, easily get caught in a rainstorm. A waterproof jacket protects against both the wet and the cold. In the past, these jackets were hardly ever used by racing cyclists during hot weather because the material could not 'breathe' and so the cyclist would sweat too heavily. Nowadays, however, it is possible to purchase waterproof jackets made from a special

A wind-jacket.

Rain-jackets with hoods.

material, Gore-Tex, which allows air to pass through, but not water. These jackets are fastened with velcro in the front and are so long at the back that they cover the saddle in order to protect the cyclist against the spray from the rear wheel. A jacket of this kind, when rolled up, will fit into a pocket of a cycling top. Waterproof leggings are useful during long rides in the rain, as indeed are rain overshoes – the latter especially so on cold, rainy days.

Equipment

A tight-fitting skin suit (as worn by Olympic champion Dill Bundi of Switzerland).

Wind Jacket and Wind Bib

Special wind jackets are manufactured which are designed for cool, blustery days. The front of these jackets is made of a wind-resistant nylon material, while the back and sleeves are made of

A thermal suit for very cold winter weather.

wool. Alternatively, you can purchase a wind bib which is worn between the vest and cycle top in order to cut down the effects of the wind on the body from exposure generated when cycling. The bib has a back and a front, but it is open at the sides to allow a certain amount of air circulation.

Skin-suit

A skin-suit is a one-piece suit with attached cycle shorts. It is fastened with a zip at the front of the suit. The material is silky smooth, man-made and clings to the body and so helps to decrease air resistance. Skin-suits are particularly popular during time trials and hill-climbing races because on such rides the cyclist does not nee pockets for food or other bits and p eces. The material is tightly woven, but the skin can breathe under it, allowing sweat to evaporate.

Two cyclists wearing the classical summer outfit on their mountain tour.

Equipment

Long cycle leggings, thermal mitts and overshoes.

Light cycle glasses giving protection against the wind – and the sun.

Thermal Suit

Thermal material which also allows the skin to breathe makes it possible for cyclists to train even in the coldest conditions. Complete suits, single jackets, bib-trousers, gloves, overshoes and hats are all available made from this material. For the incorrigible cyclist a piece of clothing somewhat akin to a diving suit is now being marketed, as are complete, all-weather suits with hood, mouth protection and waterproof sweat seams on both the jacket and the trousers – indeed everything is water- and wind-proof, but still allows the skin to breathe.

Cycle Clothing

In summer during good weather, you should train in usual cycling clothing – shorts and short-sleeved cycle top, racing shoes, short white socks and fingerless racing mitts. Cycling tops with bright, lively colours are more noticeable and improve the cyclist's safety on the road. Cyclists embarking upon long rides up and down hills or mountains should always carry a spare vest. Something as simple as ordinary newspaper positioned between the vest and cycle top by the chest is very effective in helping to avoid exposure during long descents. It is sensible to carry a waterproof jacket during changeable weather and similarly a racing cap will protect your head from the sun, while cyclists who train at high speeds should wear a helmet or at least a racing cap.

You will probably want to change into a long-sleeved cycling top during the spring and autumn and certainly in winter when the temperatures fall. You should wear two or even three cycling tops as it becomes increasingly colder

(the additional layers of air will insulate you from the cold).

When temperatures have fallen below five degrees Celsius, the cold is particularly noticeable in two areas of the body; the hands and the feet. Your hands can be protected against the cold with long-fingered mittens, woollen mittens or special thermal gloves and your feet can be protected from the cold by woollen socks pulled up over your racing shoes or by special thermal overshoes (winter-racing shoes lined with fur are now manufactured). Your head should be protected by a woollen hat which must reach over the ears, and when it turns even colder you can wear a wind-proof rain jacket over one or two jumpers. Cycle shorts and long woollen socks can be worn instead of long leggings, if preferred. Most cyclists use the above items of clothing when the temperatures have fallen to around freezing point, but only particularly enthusiastic or competitive racing cyclists train in these (or lower) temperatures; there are, of course, other sports on offer during the winter which can be exciting and satisfying.

Protective Glasses

Even the leisure cyclist reaches a speed of up to 60kmh (37mph) when cycling downhill and the racing cyclist up to 80kmh (50mph). Your eyes are vulnerable at these speeds, particularly to insects and other foreign bodies, so an increasing number of professional cyclists now wear protective racing glasses which can be clear or slightly tinted to give the additional benefit of protecting the eyes from bright sunlight.

Man and the Bicycle

The harmony between the human machine – our body, its biomechanism and its biological capacity – and the technical machine – the bicycle – is the fundamental reason for the fascination of cycling. The bodily capacity can only be fully developed when the human being and the bicycle work together perfectly. There are certain preconditions for this: the correct sitting position;

Decisive for the optimal development of performance are the cyclist's sitting position and elegant riding style.

a good cycling style; and the mastering of the art of pedalling. A good cycling style results in a simultaneous feeling of stability and lightness.

The Correct Riding Position

You can change a cyclist's sitting position by slightly adjusting both the handlebars and the saddle. This position will not be improved, however, unless the fixed points of the bicycle (the frame measurements, the length of the crank, the width of the handlebars and the stem) exactly fit the cyclist's body measurements. You can alter this sitting

position by individual adjustments to the height of the saddle, the angle of the saddle, the length of the sitting position and the height of the handlebars. During cycling you should be able to undertake every movement on the bicycle in a relaxed, easy manner. These movements will be impeded by an incorrect sitting position, which can actually lead to various medical complaints including muscle tension in the arms, the neck and the back, and pains in the upper thighs.

Indeed quite a number of professional racing cyclists who have changed from their own racing bicycle to a time-trialling machine which was not specifically made for them have

Riding Skills

had to pay for a slightly different sitting position with painful tendons, particularly in the knee joint. This demonstrates just how important your posture is when cycling.

The Height of the Saddle

The saddle should, of course, be neither too high nor too low and the knee should be neither too stretched nor too bent as the foot passes the lowest point during the pedal revolution. The angle of the knee should be approximately 170–175 degrees at this point. Initially you should adjust the saddle by guesswork but there are then three different ways finally to determine the correct height of the saddle:

1. Sit on the saddle, position the pedal at its lowest point and place your heel on the pedal. Your leg should now be stretched.
2. You should be able to slide your toes under the pedal while your foot is in a horizontal position and the pedal is at its lowest point.
3. The correct height of the saddle – measured from the centre of the bottom bracket to the top of the saddle – can be determined by multiplying your inside-leg measurement by a factor of 0.885.

Some deviations from this standard do occur; for example those cyclists who prefer to ride with a very high number of pedal revolutions usually fit their saddle a little lower. Other cyclists,

Where your legs should be positioned when you have the saddle at the correct height.

You should be able to reach the pedal comfortably with your heel when your leg is stretched.

however, such as time triallists who use more power for each pedal revolution fit their saddle a little higher and some sprinters prefer a very high saddle so that their legs are almost stretched when their foot passes the lowest point during a pedal revolution. This saddle position is much too high for a touring

Positioning of the saddle: a weight hanging from the tip of the saddle should be about 4cm behind the centre of the bottom-bracket axle.

or competitive cyclist. It is important to remember, though, that a saddle which has already been finally adjusted could have subsided by as much as 10mm after 3000–4000km cycling. It should then be readjusted.

The Positioning of the Saddle

The saddle is usually fitted so that it is horizontal, that is parallel to the top tube. It is a good idea to use a spirit level for this. Finally, the positioning of the saddle can be adjusted by sliding it backwards or forwards. The correct position is determined by letting a plumb-line fall from your knee cap; it should fall through the centre of the pedal axle when the crank is parallel to the ground. The horizontal distance between the centre of the bottom bracket and a plumb-line hanging down from the tip of the saddle is usually 2–5cm, with an average distance of 4cm (the line hangs down behind the centre of the bottom bracket). Some competitive cyclists move their saddle so that the plumb-line falling from the knee cap is closer to the centre of the bottom bracket. The distance between the tip of the saddle and the back of the handlebars, also called the sitting length, is now determined by the stem.

There should be a space of about 5mm between the bent knee and the elbow when the cranks are parallel with the down tube of the frame and the

Lowering the saddle: horizontal adjustment with a spirit-level.

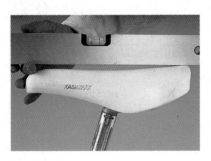

You should be able to reach under the pedal with the tips of your toes when your leg is stretched.

Correct saddle positioning: a weight hanging from the kneecap should meet the pedal axle, when the crank is in a horizontal position.

The correct length of the stem: the knee should touch the elbow in the position shown (the down position on the handlebars, crank parallel to the down tube of the frame) when both the frame measurements and the sitting position are correct.

cyclist holds the handlebars in the down position. The knee should not touch the elbow in this position. In principle, the frame should be as short as possible and the stem as long as possible as this produces optimal stability.

The frame is too short if you still need a stem in excess of 12–15cm after you have finished adjusting the saddle.

Finally, one more word of advice: if a cyclist suffers from chronic back pain, it is worth reducing the length of the stem

Forceful pedalling. The cyclist has moved slightly forward for a stronger input of power.

Riding Skills

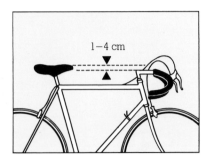

The height of the handlebars: these can be positioned at the same level as the saddle, or alternatively 3–4cm below it according to the build and fitness of the cyclist.

by 5–10mm – even if the frame is apparently the correct size and the stem the correct length.

The Height of the Handlebars

The handlebars on everyday and touring bicycles can certainly be higher than the saddle as an upright position is preferable when riding on these bicy-

cles. Indeed this results in a comfortable riding position. The more competitively you ride and the more your speed increases, the more beneficial it is to ride in a crouched position as this helps minimise air resistance. Your breathing should, however, not be affected by this, although your posture will obviously depend upon the shape of your body. Cyclists with the beginnings of a paunch will have to start with comparatively higher handlebars! The height should roughly correspond to the height of the saddle at the beginning of training, but as weight is lost, so the handlebars can be lowered in relation to the saddle.

Very fit cyclists can position their handlebars 3–4cm below the saddle level, but whatever position you adopt, you must be able to breathe properly in the down position. The angle of the ends of the handlebars should be horizontal or perhaps lean slightly towards the back.

Table of Measurements

The ideal dimensions of a racing bicycle have already been discussed (the size of the frame, the length of the stem, the length of the crank and the length of the toe-clips). You should now adjust the following measurements to your sitting position: the saddle level (the distance between the centre of the bottom bracket and the top of the saddle); the saddle positioning (the distance between the plumb-line falling from the tip of the saddle and the middle of the bottom bracket axle); the sitting length (the distance between the tip of the saddle and the back of the handlebars – where these meet the stem) and the level of the handlebars (the perpendicular distance between the top of the saddle and the top of the handlebars).

Resistances during Cycling

If you have learned to sit correctly on your bicycle you should also try to improve upon your riding skills. You need to understand some fundamental physical principles in order to be able to master a bicycle in different situations. It is particularly important to use your faculties both rationally and sensibly when cycling as the cyclist faces different types of resistance which are negligible in other sports disciplines. There are in fact three types of resistance that you must try to overcome:

1. Torsional resistance.
2. Air resistance.
3. Gravity.

On flat ground the total resistance is determined by air and torsional resistance. Gravity comes into effect during hill climbs. Cyclists who understand which factors contribute to these resistances can minimise them by taking

The sitting position.

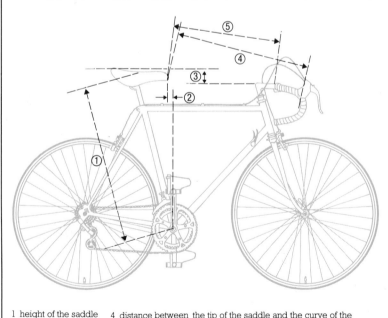

1 height of the saddle
2 saddle position
3 height of handlebars
4 distance between the tip of the saddle and the curve of the handlebars
5 distance between the tip of the saddle and the back of the handlebars

Air resistance, measured in watts, at different body positions and speeds

position	wind target (m^2)	air resistance (W)			
		30kmh	35kmh	40kmh	45kmh
high	0.5	200	300	470	650
medium	0.4	150	230	340	500
low	0.3	110	150	250	350

certain measures. This is particularly advisable because our means of counteracting these forces are limited.

Cycle Power

In science, it is common practice to measure power in kilowatts (kW) or in horsepower (hp). We are familiar with these units because we use them when discussing the power of cars. These units can also be applied to human beings and they are applicable in the following way: Human beings who are not in training generate about 2–3W for every kilogram of body-weight, that is roughly 150–250W for someone aged 30. Daily housework generates approximately 100–120W. A person who frequently climbs stairs generates 120–150W, a slow jog 150–180W, touring cyclists riding at an average speed of 25–30kmh generate 180–220W. Older or 'veteran' racing cyclists who weigh around 70kg have to generate roughly 300–350W in order to reach an average speed of 40kmh. Road racing cyclists need to be able to generate 400–450W. Professional cyclists exceed

1 horsepower (hp) = 735 watts (W) = 0.735 kilowatts (kW)
1 Kilowatt (kW) = 1,000 watts (W) = 1.36 horsepower (hp)
0.1 Kilowatts (kW) = 100 watts (W) = 0.136 horsepower (hp)

even this figure; Eddie Merckx could generate 500W! So you can see how vastly the extent of human capacity to generate power can vary depending upon fitness.

Speed, Body Position and Performance

A capacity of 150W is required if you are to reach a speed of up to 30kmh on flat ground without a head wind, bending slightly forward; 240W to reach a speed of 35kmh and 300W to reach a speed of 40kmh. A touring cyclist of average fitness with a capacity of 250W will be able to reach a speed of around 30–35kmh while riding on flat ground – and indeed he should be satisfied with this. If he wants to ride faster, he will have to rest from time to time by riding behind another cyclist where he is protected from the wind generated during cycling. The capacity of a racing cyclist during a time trial can be measured when he has to overcome the different resistances on his own. A capacity of around 300W (which must be generated over a long period of time) is needed if an average speed of 40kmh is to be attained. The average speed of 'two or three-up' time trials is approximately 50kmh nowadays so the leader has to generate over 500W while he rides in the front – almost two-thirds of one horsepower!

Riding Style

You might assume that the sitting position on a bicycle is irrelevant at low speeds but a good riding style is the very thing which makes cycling so enjoyable. Your capacity (and so your enjoyment) is markedly increased by a good riding style – even without any extra training. In fact a good riding technique is a prerequisite for success in competitive cycling. The competitive cyclist must try to minimise the 'generated resistances' and overcome them as economically as possible. There are hardly two cyclists who ride their bicycle in the same way – just as there aren't two people who walk in quite the same way; everybody has their own idiosyncracies, particularly as regards anatomy and temperament. Nevertheless, there are certain elements which characterise a good riding style, especially when it comes to body position and leg work.

Body Positions

The position of the body should ideally become increasingly aerodynamic as the cycle speed increases. You can sit upright during low speeds on an everyday bicycle or on a touring bicycle – and even on a racing bicycle with little disadvantage. However, cyclists prefer a slightly bent forward position during average speeds of around 20–30kmh and it actually becomes *necessary* to ride in a low position at speeds of 30–40kmh or more. The acceptable positions of the body differ because they create different 'wind targets'. The wind target measures about 0.5–0.6 cubic metres while sitting upright, with the handlebars held at their highest point (the upper part of the handlebars on a racing bicycle). Breathing is easy – even when the stomach is a little on the large side.

The wind target measures between

Riding Skills

0.4 and 0.5 cubic metres in the middle position in which the body leans slightly forward. Racing cyclists grip the brakes from the top in this position which is still quite comfortable.

The wind target decreases to 0.275–0.3 cubic metres when cycling in the down position in which the 'target' of the head disappears into that of the body. In this position racing cyclists hold on to the handlebars at the bottom of the curve. If you still have a stomach which is on the large side, breathing is somewhat hindered in this position.

The following example shows how important it is to be familiar with the different positions of the body and the various grips on the handlebars; a cyclist of average fitness with a capacity of 200–250W can reach a speed of 30–32kmh while sitting upright, 33–36kmh while cycling in the middle position and as much as 38–40kmh when cycling in the down position.

One final point about a good cyclist: the upper part of the body does not move at all during pedalling, in any of the three positions mentioned above. Accordingly, the handlebars are held without any kind of swaying and the cyclist rides straight ahead without any sideways movement. The arms should be slightly bent in order to absorb shocks from the road. Someone with a good technique should always feel relaxed on the bicycle, and

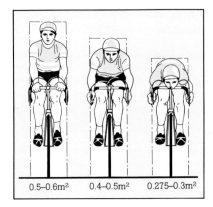

Wind-target areas at different positions on a racing bicycle.

0.5–0.6m²	0.4–0.5m²	0.275–0.3m²

consciously loosen the muscles of the arms, shoulders and neck. It is very important to keep working at a perfect riding style; deviations are very hard to lose once they have become a habit. There is nothing to riding fast and without rests – anyone can do it. What must be learned initially is to ride slowly, in a relaxed manner and with a perfect riding style. An incorrect riding style prevents a cyclist from ever reaching the potential of his capacity.

Legwork

The legs should move close to the frame in parallel either side of the frame. The knees may actually brush the top tube of the frame without affecting your technique. This ideal legwork is only possible if the feet are properly fitted on to the pedals. The instep of the foot should be positioned exactly above the pedal axle – particularly important for pedals without toe-clips. If toe-clips are fitted, they should be of a length to fit your size of racing shoes and ideally there should be a gap of about 2mm between the toe-clip and the racing shoe in order to avoid chafing or rubbing of the shoe. Racing cyclists who use proper racing shoes with toe-clips should carry out these fine adjustments once the shoe is positioned on the pedal. One other important point is to ensure that the length of the shoe is parallel to the frame. The toes of the shoes should never point outwards – if anything a little inwards. The feet will only then be able to work in a line parallel to the frame. This is an essential prerequisite for an optimal cycling style.

Course of Motion

You should work towards a perfect riding style with a parallel leg movement even when cycling on an everyday or touring bicycle. It looks odd – and is biomechanically disadvantageous – if you push the pedals with the centre of your foot or with your heels, or if you cycle with your toes pointing outwards and your legs apart. There are three factors which should be checked frequently until the perfect riding style has been reached:

1. The legs should always work in parallel with the leg actions close to the

The position of the foot on the pedal: the instep of the foot should be positioned exactly over the pedal axle.

There should be a space of 2–3mm between the toe-clip and the shoe.

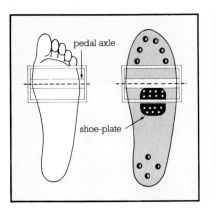

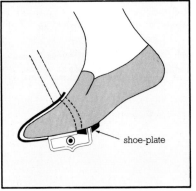

Urs Freuler, one of the best professional cyclists in the world, standing up to ride uphill.

Riding Skills

frame. There should be barely any room between the knees and the top tube; women prefer this style instinctively – men have to learn it.

2.   A perfect stylist will do all the work with their legs – the rest of the body remains still. Neither the head nor the upper part of the body should sway except in very competitive situations such as a climb or a sprint.

3.   The leg power should be distributed evenly over the pedal during cycling.

Pedal-action

The most important action in cycling, and one which must constantly be relearned, is correct pedalling. It might seem surprising that cyclists need to learn a skill that they believe they have already mastered, but very few are familiar with the principles essential for the perfect round pedal-action – or if they are, they are even less likely to make proper use of them. Even professional cyclists have to work at the perfect, round pedal-action at the beginning of every year in order to relearn (or perhaps revise) it. This should be a comfort to all cyclists!

The power which moves the bicycle forwards is transferred to the pedals from the lower limbs and then transmitted over the cranks, bottom bracket, chainwheels, chain, freewheel, rear hub and the rear wheel. Put very basically, the lower limbs are made up of the following structures: upper thighs; lower legs; and feet, all of which are connected by joints and bend and stretch depending upon whether the appropriate muscles contract or relax.

From a purely technical point of view, pedalling is an interaction between three levers; from a physiological point of view, however, it is the result of certain muscle contractions. The first of the three levers is the upper thigh. The hip joint connects it to the pelvis, which is static while sitting on the saddle. The upper thigh is connected to the lower leg at the knee joint and carries out a regular up-and-down movement during pedalling through the bending and stretching of the hip joint.

The second lever is the lower leg, which begins at the knee joint and ends at the ankle joint.

The third lever is the foot which is connected to the lower leg at the ankle joint. The power is transmitted from the instep of the foot to the shoe and the pedal in which process the foot carries out a relaxed up-and-down movement through the ankle joint.

Nature developed the lower limbs for running and walking – but they are, of course, also very suitable for pedalling, although this must be learned through constant practice (as, indeed, must running) in order to convert the maximum amount of energy into forward motion by using the minimum amount of power. This ideal skill can only be mastered if the rules for a good riding style are adhered to; someone who pedals perfectly moves only their lower limbs in parallel close to the frame of the bicycle while keeping the rest of their body quite motionless (particularly the upper part of the body, the head and the arms).

When you master this skill you will now have to move on to perhaps a yet more important point, that is the ability to transmit power evenly from the feet on to the pedals during the entire pedal revolution, ideally throughout the 360 degrees of the revolution. Cyclists who simply push the pedals from the 'top' to the 'bottom' utilise only about a quarter of the complete revolution. Besides, the result is an erratic style of very low efficiency. The pressure and then the pull of this movement should be carried out evenly and always point towards the bottom bracket. It is, however, impossible to reach this technological ideal because the size and direction of the forces which need to be developed by nature change at each point of the pedal revolution, although someone who has excellent technique will manage to get quite close to this ideal. The closer your style can be to this, the better a cyclist you will be.

The illustration on the following page shows the ideal pedal revolution. The forces working on the pedals have been shown as 'power parallelograms' in twelve successive positions of the pedal. The ideal direction of the power is shown by the bold arrow A–B which runs at an angle of 90 degrees to the crank position. This ideal direction is a result of the two kinds of power, arrow A–C (vertical power) and A–D (horizontal power). Vertical power is applied through downward pressure or upward pull; horizontal power is ap-

The round pedal-action: you only use a small part of the entire pedalling action if you only push the pedal down. You can decisively increase the effectiveness of pedalling by lifting and lowering the tip of the toes – with a corresponding foreward pressure and backward pull.

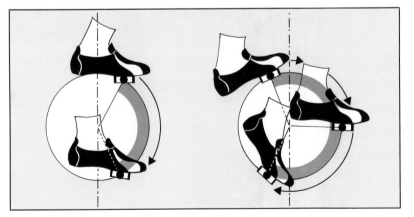

plied through forward or backward pressure and pull. Cyclists who do not possess a natural talent for pedalling should always remind themselves of the different stages involved in a pedal revolution.

Stage 1. Top dead centre. Applying vertical power has no effect whatsoever. Only one type of power directed to the front – preferably perpendicularly to the crank – will move the pedal forward. The toes have to be lifted in order to generate power through the extensor muscles of the upper thigh and the flexors of the foot which together push the pedals forwards.

Stage 2. The horizontal power needed to force the pedal forwards decreases and the vertical power from top to bottom starts to become effective.

Stage 3. The vertical power is now greater than the forward pushing power. The level of the foot is nearly horizontal and the toes are only slightly lifted.

Stage 4. Vertical power is the only effective power at this point.

Stage 5. Vertical power is at this stage already combined with certain horizontal powers generated by the flexor muscles at the back of the upper thighs as well as the muscles of the buttocks.

Stage 6. The traction towards the back of the pedal revolution is now more powerful than the vertical force pushing downwards. The toes have to point down in order to make this possible.

Stage 7. Bottom dead centre. A horizontal force towards the back of the pedal is the only effective power at this point. Pressure from top to bottom is wholly ineffective. The foot has to be stretched downwards in the ankle joint as far as possible, the toes have to point down. The upper thigh starts to bend in the hip joint.

Stage 8. The power towards the back remains necessary and an additional vertical force upwards is now required.

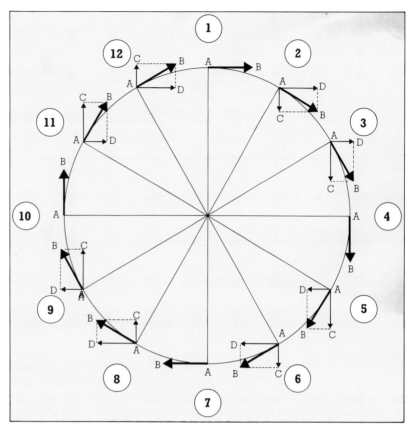

Forces during pedalling: horizontal (A–D) and vertical (A–C) forces must be at a certain ratio during every phase of the pedalling action so that the resulting power (A–B) is at a maximum. The length of the arrows indicates the amount of power. You can see that the most effective lever always runs perpendicularly to the crank.

The toes still point down. The upper thigh, bent in the hip joint, is lifted.

Stage 9. The upward pull increases further and now exceeds the backward pressure.

Stage 10. Vertical power upwards is the only effective power at this point.

Stage 11. The pedal is pulled further upwards, whereupon a tractive effect forwards is required.

Stage 12. The power working forwards should exceed that of the upward pull at this point. This can either have a tractive effect with downward-pointing toes (for a high frequency of pedal revolutions) or a pushing effect with upward pointing toes (a low frequency of pedal revolutions).

If the powers are distributed over the entire pedal revolution in this way two distinct goals are achieved.

1. The direction power, A–B, which results from the combination of horizontal and vertical powers is always most effective at an angle of 90 degrees to the crank. This is the only way in which to achieve the optimal efficiency.

2. Every muscle in the region of the hips, upper thighs, lower legs and feet is used in turn in an ideal interaction, so utilising every possible power.

During pedalling the most important part of the body is the foot. It constantly moves up and down around the axle of

Riding Skills

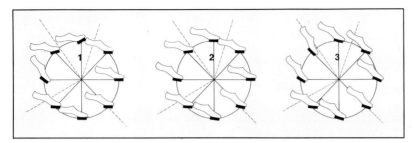

The round pedal-action at different pedalling frequencies. 1 A low number of pedal revolutions (60–90 a minute, for example during climbs, cycling in mountains, time trialling and so forth); conscious lifting of the tip of the toes at the top dead centre and lowering of the toes at the bottom dead centre. 2 A medium number of pedal revolutions (90–110 a minute during relaxed training, cycling in a bunch, cycle racing and so forth); the foot is nearly horizontal at the top and bottom dead centres. 3 A high number of pedal revolutions (110–150 revolutions a minute or more, for instance during sprints, intensive endurance training and so forth); the tips of the toes are more or less pointing downwards during all phases. Top and bottom dead centres are passed with power.

the ankle joint and the toes point alternately up and down.

The foot needs to be relaxed, supple and mobile in the ankle joint for this to be possible. This movement of the foot is most extreme during hill climbs and long stretches on the flat when there is a high frequency of pedal revolutions. The higher the number of revolutions, the less time remains for the lifting of the toes near the top dead centre. The position of the foot becomes increasingly horizontal and may even point downwards constantly during a very high frequency of pedal revolutions.

The best way to learn the perfect round pedal-action is consciously to carry out the actions of the ankle joint and observe them. Initially this is best practised by slow pedal revolutions using minimum power. The speed of the pedal revolutions is subsequently increased while still trying to maintain the relaxed movement of the ankle joint (indeed only possible when the foot moves in a completely relaxed manner).

It is a good idea to practise the round pedal-action with one foot at a time. Withdraw your left foot from the toe-clip, for instance, and turn the pedal with your right foot only, trying to move the pedal as evenly as possible. You

will be able to determine what is effective and necessary to power this movement. Next change the foot after a few hundred metres and practise with the other. You will notice how much your feeling for the round pedal-action has increased when you once again pedal using both feet. The interaction of both legs should be practised as soon as you have mastered pedalling with each leg separately. It is most important to ensure that the leg which is supposed to pull the pedal up is properly lifted. Remember; a leg weighs around 12–15kg and this means that it constitutes up to 20 per cent of your total body-weight. The result of pushing down one pedal with the weight of the leg plus an active force of 10kg results in the power of 22–25kg. A force corresponding to the weight of one leg is therefore lost if one foot is rested on the pedal – so that an active pressure equivalent to only 10kg is applied. Accordingly, it is most important not to let the foot on the upward-turning pedal rest, but to perform an *active* upward pull (this is, of course, only possible if the foot is fixed to the pedal).

The 'quality' of a cyclist is not determined by the power with which they can push down the pedals, but rather the ability to conduct the pedal revolutions which are relaxed, round and fast.

This is particularly the case on the flat. Additional power will, of course, be applied if a cyclist breaks away from a bunch during sprinting or hill climbs. Nevertheless, the relaxed movement of the feet should remain a greater priority than power – even during climbs.

A figure of 50–60 pedal revolutions per minute is usually suggested for leisure cyclists, but this number is too small for competitive cyclists since it does not allow any level of endurance – because the input of power is too great.

Cycling is essentially not a kind of power sport but an endurance sport. Racing cyclists usually turn their pedals over at 90–110 revolutions per minute while racing and training and as much as 120–150 during track racing. Every world record has been achieved with pedal revolutions exceeding 100 per minute. The leisure cyclist, too, should aim for roughly this figure. An ability to push the pedal in a relaxed, round and economic fashion with a revolution frequency of this order must be learned through a great deal of practice. As part of this learning process, it is advisable to cycle with a small number of pedal revolutions over a long period of time. Even top professional racing cyclists have to practise this perfect round pedal-action with a low frequency of pedal revolutions (perhaps 42/17 or 42/18) during training in winter and spring while covering around 1,000–5,000km – before returning to the training camp where they continue to practise the perfect round pedal-action.

Training with a high input of power follows later – just before and during the race period. Some cyclists practise the round pedal-action with a fixed wheel (that is a rear wheel without a freewheel). A fixed wheel requires constant cycling without interruption and means that it is imperative to pedal in an even, smooth manner as otherwise the ride becomes erratic and the cyclist bumps up and down on the saddle! Every bicycle can in fact be equipped with a fixed wheel. A suitable freewheel with perhaps 17 teeth will need to be attached to the rear wheel and the chain shortened so that it is just long enough to fit around the small chainwheel in the front. Cyclists who cover a distance of 1,000–1,500km in this way will, if nothing else, get the feeling for the correct pedal action. The movement can subsequently be practised further by using the usual hub.

It should be obvious that the perfect, round pedal-action is a science in itself. Patient, constant practice is needed until you have learned this skill inside out. Only then can you truly claim to know how to cycle.

A powerful riding style just before the finish (Hans Hindelang).

Riding Skills

Good Cycling Technique

Once you have mastered both the correct sitting position and a good pedalling action, you will need to become familiar with various road conditions and types of rural terrain in order to overcome, as effectively as possible, the three different types of resistance mentioned earlier. This is especially important when cycling at speed. Also of the utmost importance is safety – and this, too, demands good riding skills to lessen the likelihood of accidents.

Cornering

High speeds are attained during cycling, particularly when riding downhill. If you turn corners too fast you can easily be forced out into the road or have a fall if the pedal on the inside of the curve touches the ground. It can, of course, also be dangerous to apply the brakes at the wrong point. The racing cyclist has to turn every corner at maximum speed and accordingly should not underestimate the danger simply because he encounters them so frequently. The correct cornering technique is most important – add a certain element of speed and it becomes vital. When turning corners centrifugal force pulls the bicycle outwards. The following forces are involved when measuring the centrifugal force for each corner:

m = mass, measured in kilograms
r = radius of the corner
w = speed while turning the corner

The relationship between the centrifugal force, F_z, and the other variables is as follows:

$$F_z = m \times \frac{w^2}{r}$$

The following principles can now be deduced:

1. The centrifugal force increases in proportion to the combined weight of the cyclist and his bicycle.
2. The centrifugal force increases in proportion to the square of the speed.
3. The centrifugal force increases in inverse proportion to the radius of the curve, that is the tighter the corner, the greater the centrifugal force.

However, the centrifugal force generated by a particular corner can be minimised by leaning the body and the bicycle into it and for this the body of the cyclist needs to be as stable as possible on the bicycle. The leg on the outside of the corner must be straightened in order to increase the stability by increasing the pressure on the outside pedal. The stability on a racing bicycle can be further increased by holding the handlbars in the down position. Obviously, you should turn the handlebars less, the higher your speed is. This also means that the leaning of the cyclist and bicycle into the corner must be increased when cycling at a higher speed. When cornering, your angle should be no more acute (no smaller) than 73 degrees on dry tarmac and around 80 degrees on concrete. If the angle is reduced beyond this there is a danger of the wheels slipping. Cyclist and bicycle should ideally be positioned at the same angle but there is another technique in which the upper part of the body remains more upright than the bicycle.

Finally, you can lean towards the inside of the curve with the upper part of the body and stretch the leg on the same side in towards the curve. This last technique should, however, not become a habit and should only be used in an emergency when, for instance, you realise that you are turning the corner at too high a speed. The leg which is stretched out and away from the bicycle acts as an additional counterweight against the centrifugal force which otherwise would be too powerful.

Brakes should be applied *before* the corner, and not in the corner itself. It is also advantageous to slide back in the saddle slightly in order to add pressure above the back wheel while turning. You should bear in mind that the grip of highly pressurised tyres is minimised during descents as well as on wet or sandy surfaces.

The centrifugal forces can be decreased, if your 'route' around a corner runs in such a way that you can in-

The position of a cyclist turning a corner. 1 The body is at the same angle as the bicycle (the usual position when taking corners). 2 The body is bent inwards, the knee points towards the corner and the bicycle is more upright than the body. 3 The bicycle leans further into the corner than the body, the knee points towards the corner.

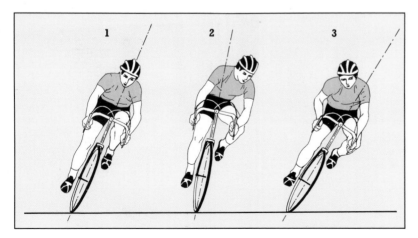

crease the radius of the corner by cycling wide; it is, of course, only permissable to turn corners in this manner if the roads are closed for a cycle race. The radius of left turns can only be increased as far as the road markings showing the centre, but you should at least leave a gap of about one metre at the near edge in order to be able to avoid obstacles.

If you suddenly encounter gravel or loose chippings while cornering you should immediately sit upright for some moments, cycle straight ahead and only then apply the brakes – it is very dangerous to brake while leaning in towards the corner. If you are racing in a bunch, you should attempt to cycle ahead before a corner in order to determine the ideal route around it; it is always worth trying to keep to the inside of the corner, if it is not possible to reach the front. Riding at the outside of a corner, you run the risk of being pushed off your bicycle by another falling cyclist.

A cornering technique has to be developed slowly; initially try cycling in slalom style with various sideways bends (along a straight road). If you can perform this skill in a relaxed and secure manner, you should practise it with the correct pedal revolutions. The pedal inside the curve should always be lifted.

It is vital that cyclists should keep in

Cornering technique: the body and the racing bicycle are at one angle and the inside pedal is pulled up.

Riding Skills

to the left around corners. They should not go too wide around corners nor 'attack' them. You must also be sure that both tyres are securely fixed to the rims on racing bicycles!

Hill Climbs and Descents

There are basically four different styles of hill cycling:

1. A hill climb while standing up ('honking').
2. A Hill climb while sitting down and holding the handlebars in the top position.
3. A hill climb while sitting down and holding on to the brake levers.
4. A hill descent in the low, aerodynamic position.

Honking

The entire body is used in an athletic way during honking. The aim is to make the best possible use of body-weight and power input. The body-weight is transferred to the stretched leg while the arms and the upper part of the body pull at the handlebars. This results in the bicycle swaying from left to right and the upper part of the body remaining vertical. As the left leg presses the pedal down, the right hand

Mountain climbing using the top position of the handlebars.

pushes the handlebars down and the left pulls it up so that the bicycle swings to the right. The handlebars are usually held around the brake levers.

Cyclists 'honk' during steep or long climbs and when they attempt to break away from a bunch during races. Hill specialists, or 'climbers', are able to cover very long hill stretches riding in this manner. A technique of alternately honking and sitting down can prevent early tiring as the two styles use different sets of muscles. Some climbers such as the Spaniard Frederico Bahamontes, known as the 'Toledo Eagle', change from honking to sitting and vice versa after a certain number of pedal revolutions during long uphill stretches or mountain climbing and vice versa. Everyone must find their own rhythm while cycling uphill.

The fact that a cyclist also needs well developed muscles in the arms and the upper part of the body is apparent during honking. For novices the most difficult aspect of this riding style is to distribute the body-weight evenly; the rear wheel can slip if the body's centre of gravity is positioned too far forwards. Conversely, the cyclist's body-weight is not fully used if the centre of gravity is positioned too far back as this makes it impossible to use the muscles of the arms and the trunk properly. Hence honking must form part of any training programme. It is a skill frequently used during racing – so it is important to master it.

Hill Descents

When cycling downhill novices should concentrate on a safe cornering technique rather than speed. Nevertheless it is interesting to see how racing cyclists start their descent after finishing a climb; they will suddenly start to push hard just before the top, gain speed and change into a high gear on the top of the hill. They then start their descent

Bernard Hinault at the head of the pack during the Tour de Suisse.

Riding Skills

An efficient body position is possible by holding the brake-levers where they meet the handlebars.

in a high gear and push the pedals so fast that pedalling seems to become impossible.

The cyclists must then adopt an aerodynamic position during the descent; they lean forwards, tuck in the elbows and press the knees on to the frame. Feet, pedals and cranks are all positioned vertically in order to minimise wind resistance. The head is bent forward towards the neck and the eyes look straight ahead so that the course can be scanned. You can often make some sort of recovery during a descent because the speed is usually maintained by the power of gravity which pulls the bicycle downhill, without turning the pedals. Concentration, however, must be intense as speeds in excess of 60–80kmh are frequently reached. Obstacles must be spotted as soon as possible and then avoided!

Corners have to be turned with perfect technique and the speed, the angle of corners, the surface of the road and the grip of the tyres must all be weighed up constantly during a descent. The leg muscles should remain relaxed, particularly during long descents. From time to time one leg and then the other should be stretched (as well as easy forward and backward pedal movements). The aim of these

movements is twofold; to relax the muscles and to ward off the effects of exposure because the muscles are indeed exposed to the significant wind generated during cycling – as are the joints in the leg. Relaxing the leg muscles (and joints) means that the pedals can be turned as fast as necessary when the bottom of the hill is reached.

Slipstreaming

The air resistance increases in proportion to the square of the speed but, put simply, cyclists create an area behind them of noticeably lower air resistance – the slipstream. Cyclists who ride in the slipstream of another save around about forty per cent power. Seen from another point of view, the leading cyclist has to generate 60–70 per cent more power than the followers! These figures sound incredible but they have been scientifically proven. This explains how relatively weak cyclists can often achieve surprisingly good results when they succeed in slipstreaming behind other cyclists to the finish – with a chance of their winning if their sprinting is good.

Cyclists who specialise in slipstreaming are, understandably, not very popular so it is a general rule amongst cyclists that everybody takes

A mountain descent in the down position of the handlebars.

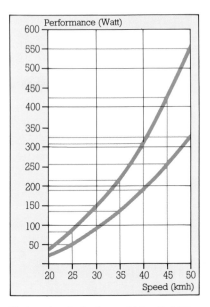

Slipstreaming: the leading cyclist (top line) has to use significantly more power than the cyclist riding in his slipstream (lower line).

a turn in leading when riding in a group. The same theory means that it is usually impossible to shrug off a cyclist who is slipstreaming – because of the extra effort this would require. You need to be cunning to shake off another cyclist by, for instance, cycling in 'slalom-style' all of a sudden so that the other cyclist is exposed to maximum air resistance. In fact you really only have a chance to shake off a 'slipstreamer' when there is reduced air resistance – during climbs or when there is a tail wind. Usually, however, cyclists take it in turn to lead (this is actually an honour when touring). The following points should be borne in mind when sitting on someone's wheel.

Followers should, in principle, always leave a 'sideways' gap of 5–15cm between the front wheel of the bicycle and the rear wheel of the bicycle in front (that is you should not follow directly behind a cyclist). This is the only way for you to scan the road ahead and avoid any obstacles. This slight shift to the side of the rider in front also allows the follower to compensate for irregularities in the speed or direction of the leader without having to apply the brakes – for repeated braking and regaining of speed is an unnecessary loss of power.

As a general rule, the cyclist who has finished leading breaks away to the side in the direction of the wind, leaving the person behind to take over the leadership. Allowing an additional distance of 30–40cm (perhaps 50–60cm for novices) between the rear wheel of the leader and the front wheel of the first follower has proved to be worth while both because misunderstandings about the wind direction – and so the direction in which a cyclist is expected to break away – have arisen, and because you cannot be entirely sure that novices will always abide by this rule. Accidents occur all too frequently when novices do not follow this rule, riding too close to the leader and falling when he breaks away in the wrong direction, or perhaps their wheel touching the leader's.

Slipstreaming requires constant concentration; you should never daydream but rather remain alert and maintain concentration. This is easier to achieve if you change the focus of your attention, for example from the bottom bracket, to the legs and to the back of the cyclist ahead and then back again. You will ride in a more relaxed manner if the point on which you focus is further afield. The safety of slipstreaming increases with practice so that the distance between the two machines can gradually decrease.

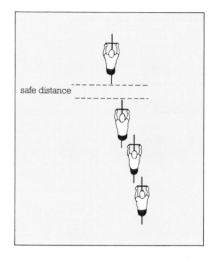

Slipstreaming at a safe distance: it is good advice for novices – as it is for every cyclist – to follow the leading cyclist not only at an angle but also at a safe distance.

The slipstreaming of a pack during a race.

Riding Skills

Group Cycling

The fun and enjoyment of riding in a group is an essential part of cycling, as it is in many sports. The effect of the slipstream, of course, is marked in cycling because of the high speed and this will encourage group cycling. Stronger cyclists will tend to take over the leadership within a group of mixed-ability cyclists and those of less prowess will also be able to keep up a reasonable speed thanks to the benefits of slipstreaming.

General Rules of Positioning

The positioning of the cyclists in a group depends upon the direction of the wind. The cyclists must be staggered if there is a strong side wind blowing to allow them to take advantage of the lee, even in windy conditions. In principle the current leader

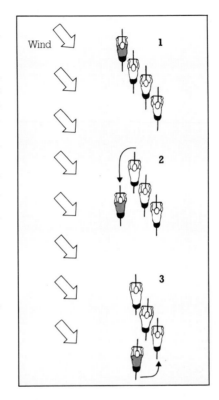

Cycling in a group; the echelon always faces the direction of the wind and the leader also always breaks away in the direction of the wind.

must fight the air resistance on his or her own, through increased work capacity, and he or she must also keep an eye open to ensure the correct route is taken since the leader is partly 'responsible' for the following cyclists. Leaders should always ride around obstacles, such as parked cars, pot-holes and so forth in a wide curve and give the other cyclists a visible warning.

When relinquishing the role of front rider, the leader will break away from the group in the direction of the wind and take up a position at the back of the group. How long the leadership lasts depends upon the power capacity of the current leader, the wind conditions and the speed. The pressure upon the

Concentration is required when cycling in a group.

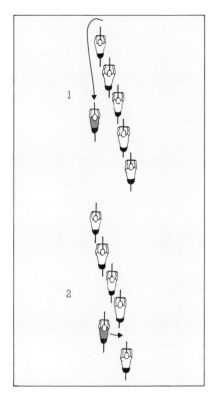

Cycling in a group. Novices should remain at the back of the group making room for the cyclist moving back into position after leading.

leader increases, of course, in proportion to the speed – and so the duration of the leadership will decrease. This is preferable to the situation in which the leader becomes so tired that he or she is slowing the group down. The cyclist who takes over the leadership must cycle at the same speed as the previous leader so that the group can maintain their rhythm. The transition between slipstreaming and leadership should always be carried out without losing speed, which requires fine judgement in both pedalling and pedalling speed. In fact, the manoeuvre demands perfection in the art of pedalling.

Novices and weak cyclists should avoid taking the lead if they are riding in a strong pack and should remain at the back of the group. The current leader should always be unimpeded and offered space, whenever their stint at the front is over and they are making

their way to the back. In this way novice cyclists can familiarise themselves with the cycling in a pack.

Special Techniques

Some other techniques are also used while racing in a group, including: double row; Belgian row (or circle); and cycling on the wind-edge.

The Double Row

Cyclists ride in pairs in a double row in such a way that two single lines are created. Broadly speaking, the same rules apply as when slipstreaming in a single row. However, the change-over in the front of the bunch has to be undertaken in a different fashion; the current leaders signal to each other, speed up in order to break away from the bunch and then pull out to the sides (the cyclist on the right to the right and the cyclist on the left to the left) before moving to the back of the bunch. The two cyclists do not move out at the same angle but diagonally – in order to leave room for the other riders further down the line (*see* illustration). Larger groups of cyclists out on a training ride usually cycle in double rows (British law permits this so long as they are not a danger to other road users).

Belgian Row or Circle

This technique is demanding and is not mastered by every racing cyclist. None the less, it is particularly useful for small groups who wish to ride at a high speed. This system is basically formed from two single lines in which the cyclists change their position up one line and down the other in a circular fashion, so supplying one another 'with slipstream'. The crucial difference between this technique and the double row is that there is only one leader at the front of the pack. The cyclist immediately behind the leader overtakes him or her. The cyclist who has just

overtaken takes up his position just ahead of the previous leader, the exact place being determined by the wind direction until this cyclist, in turn, is overtaken by the next pursuer.

This absorbing group work means that each cyclist always rides in the slipstream of the person in front – except, of course, when they happen to be leading the group. The two lines of cyclists carry out circular movements in this way, the line which is moving back from the front of the group moving more slowly than that moving towards it. This 'Belgian row' or 'Belgian circle' must be thoroughly practised before it can be used in a race.

Cycling two abreast; changeover to the outside, one cyclist a little ahead of the other.

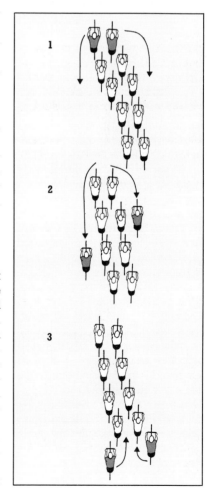

Riding Skills

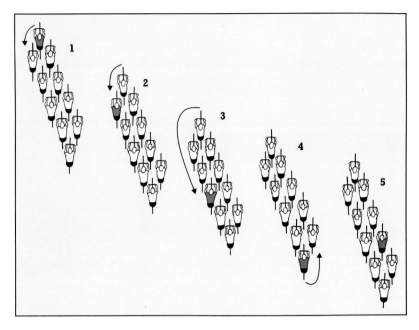

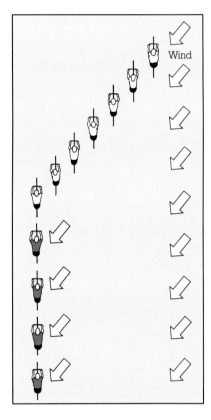

The Belgian Row or 'circle'. The leading cyclist overtakes the cyclist to his left (1). He then gently drops back in the group to the left (2) before dropping further back in the group (3). He then changes over to the right at the end of the group (4) and moves towards the front again in the right-hand row (5).

Formation Cycling in the Wind

The group of cyclists should be staggered whenever the wind blows towards them at an angle. This formation, also called an 'echelon', should only extend as far as the centre of the road when training but may take up the entire road in a race on closed roads. Those cyclists who do not manage to take up a place within this staggered formation are left riding in the wind in a very unfortunate position; they are unable to take advantage of riding in the slipstream of another cyclist. This results in increased effort and a loss of power. The cyclists riding in the wind will soon lose their strength if the leading group co-operate and maintain or increase their speed – the cyclists riding in the wind will be unable to keep up. The best means of coping with a situation of this kind is to form a second staggered formation which can follow the first group at a certain distance. This results in a number of echelons being formed.

Overcoming Obstacles

When cycling at high speed you should always remain alert – particularly when on a racing cycle. The winding of the road, the direction of the wind, the cyclist in front, the traffic and the road surface must all be constantly checked. Innumerable obstacles such as potholes, road-works, large stones and sticks will crop up and so you must know how to overcome obstacles properly – from the very start of your training. Wide ditches and railway lines are overcome by riding across them diagonally and short, gritty stretches or soft, muddy patches are best tackled by a burst of speed. You should also take into account that there will be a slight loss of grip on damp, slippery or oily road surfaces.

The best way to deal with pot-holes, narrow ditches, stones and the like is to lift the front tyre by rising from the saddle, positioning the cranks horizontally,

Cycling in the wind. The wind is blowing from the right and so the cyclists are staggered to the left. The cyclists in dark shirts were unable to find a place in the staggering and are riding in the wind. The wind resistance is much larger for these cyclists than those who found a place in the staggering.

Overcoming obstacles; cycling through a ditch (1 correct, 2 incorrect).

gripping the handlebars firmly and pulling them upwards suddenly and forcefully. It is best to practise this action by riding up and down kerbs. You can also lift the rear wheel off the ground by leaning the body forwards over the handlebars and pulling the pedals upwards. Indeed, it is quite possible to undertake jumps of 1.5–2m at a speed of 35kmh when these two ac-

tions are carried out simultaneously. The bicycle will be lifted off the ground to a height of 25–30cm. For this, you must hold the handlebars firmly and exactly straight in order to avoid a fall. You should initially practise this at medium speed, so that jumps of 10–15cm are achieved. The pulling up of the front wheel and the carrying out of small jumps with a racing bicycle are

all part of the perfect cycling technique; you have greater control over your actions, are more familiar with the capabilities of your bicycle and know that you are able to react quickly when sudden dangers arise.

Cycling in a group, two abreast, at high speed while holding lower parts of the handlebars.

be achieved if your knees lean towards the frame and the cranks are in a horizontal position. Once your confidence has grown, you could attempt to ride in small curves.

Another benefit of cycling upright – without holding the handlebars – is that you are able to breathe more efficiently – your thorax is most 'flexible' when sitting upright with your arms hanging down at your side (more flexible even than the customary position of holding your arms up above your head as adopted in breathing exercises). The muscles of the arms, shoulders and neck will relax when cycling upright with your arms hanging down by your side.

Avoiding Injury

The most common causes of cycling accidents and injuries – particularly during road races and training – are as follows:

1. Cycling too fast.
2. Poor road surface and the nature of the route.
3. Weather conditions.
4. Mechanical faults.
5. Cyclists being bunched too tightly.
6. Lack of training and/or experience.

The relentless concentration needed when following closely behind another bicycle another makes great demands on a cyclist, particularly so on a novice. Concentration tends to diminish as exhaustion sets in. Consequently it is important that a cyclist is in good condition and can therefore concentrate over long periods; if you cycle to the limit of your ability you are less likely to be able to react quickly. You must also master the technique of sitting on someone's wheel while allowing sufficient lateral distance and also a safe distance in front of you.

Cycling without holding on to the handlebars needs to be practised. It promotes relaxation and is, as you can see, necessary during races when eating and drinking.

No-hands Cycling

It is never advisable to ride a bicycle without holding on to the handlebars in traffic. It is, however, useful to let go of the handlebars on an empty road and to let your arms hang loosely at your side while sitting upright. This helps

you recover during a longer cycle ride, relaxes the muscles in the back and helps improve your sense of balance; it also gives you a better idea of how your particular bicycle handles. Once again you should initially attempt to ride in this manner over a very short distance – just a few metres – and be very careful, avoiding any corners. A more stable cycling style will

Accidents are usually unnecessary – they can be avoided through proper conduct.

Injuries

The following injuries are quite common during falls:

1. Superficial grazes.
2. Fractured collar-bones.
3. Concussion.

Grazes are invariably dirty from the dust on the road and so every cyclist should have a tetanus inoculation. He or she should also use a crash-hat or helmet in order to avoid head injuries.

The only other types of injury worth mentioning here are strains of the spine (particularly common in young people) and of the knee. The base of the spine is sometimes overworked even in such manoeuvres as changing a riding style or sitting position. To help prevent this, every cyclist (particularly younger cyclists) should perform stretching exercises designed to strengthen the spine.

Strains of the knee joint can usually be traced back either to excessive pressure on the knee-cap or too strong a pull of the tendon connecting the muscles of the upper thigh to the lower leg. The gear ratio should not be too high too soon as this is likely to cause this type of injury, especially in young cyclists. Initially, maximum power is best avoided.

Cycling, however, does not lead to joint problems such as arthritis – even for professional racing cyclists, who cover around 300,000km over a period of ten years, that is 50 million pedal rotations! This, surely, is evidence that cycling is gentle on the joints.

Traffic Rules and Regulations

Traffic rules must, of course, be obeyed by cyclists. You must observe traffic lights and rights of way and, to state the obvious, cyclists should not bump into each other on the roads or cycle paths. A good cyclist is always alert for other traffic and possible hazards and is prepared to yield to other users of the road, even if they are in the wrong. After all, what good is it being in the right if you still end up in hospital? You must develop a feeling for different traffic situations and should not take for granted that a car turning left will necessarily see you. You should be ready to brake when approaching traffic lights even if they are green. Overtaking cars and lorries is a common cause of accidents because the drivers do not usually expect a cyclist to be in that position. Cyclists are frequently not seen by motorists because they are riding in the blind spot of their mirror. It

Children should learn how to cycle correctly in traffic at an early age.

is very important to look behind you when cycling – whatever type of event (competition, training or leisure) you are taking part in. After you have ridden a bicycle for a while you develop a feeling for what is going on behind you although you must still look around from time to time in order to make sure your intuition was correct. It is also essential to look behind you when turning right to ensure you can carry out this manoeuvre safely.

Parents and Children

Between seven and ten thousand children are injured in cycle accidents every year in the United Kingdom. One of the reasons for this is that too many parents allow their children to cycle on the road too soon. Children do not necessarily know the traffic regulations even if they can ride a bicycle well. A 5-year-old is unable to assess speed and distance – and their reactions are not the same as those of an adult. Children must not be allowed to cycle in traffic before they have reached the age of eleven. At this age they should be able to balance, cycle straight ahead, use the handlebars correctly, look to the left and the right, apply the brakes correctly, perceive dangers in good time and act upon them. Parents should also realise the following facts:

1. Children are not necessarily familiar with traffic rules and regulations even if they have been taught them at school. Parents should assume too little rather than too much knowledge on this matter.
2. The safest route for children should be chosen jointly by parents and their children before they set out.
3. Parents should always ensure that every part of the bicycle is in working order, including: the bell; the brakes; front and rear lights; and (if fitted) reflectors in the spokes and on the pedals. The tyres should always be well pumped up and must not be worn.

Riding Skills

The chain should not be too loose and the handlebars, saddle, pedals, carrier and dynamo should always be screwed on tightly.

The Competitive Cyclist in Traffic

It is unsafe to ride either a racing bicycle or BMX machine without lights or reflectors in road traffic. In the United Kingdom, all cyclists must fit their machines with lights and reflectors when riding in the dark. All cyclists should always be particularly considerate on the road and set a good example.

Some cycle paths may cause problems for competitive cyclists because pedestrians may be alarmed by the rapid – and silent – approach of a racing cycle (the speed of a competitive cyclist on a cycle path is comparable to that of a moped). Accordingly, it can be difficult to decide whether to ride on the cycle path or on the road. Every cyclist when riding on the road should follow certain rules: the distance between the bicycle and the kerb (or the edge of the road) should always be around 80cm, so that you have room for manoeuvre if a car or lorry drives past too closely; you must always watch the traffic situation closely; and be aware of what is happening both in front and behind you so that you can anticipate any traffic developments and respond to them.

You should overtake a stationary vehicle to the right by cycling towards the centre of the road in good time and passing the vehicle *slowly* – the driver might fling open the door without looking back.

You should ride slowly past a traffic jam and when cycling in a group on a busy road, you should ride in single file – two abreast only when riding on a quiet road. The leading cyclist of a group should always remember that a group takes longer to cross a road than a single cyclist.

If you have an electronic speedometer or computer you should not switch it on until you have left the built-up area. Otherwise you might be tempted to cycle too fast in town and ignore traffic regulations – just in order to keep your average speed high! In any case, it is not particularly healthy or effective to train at high speeds in town because of the exhaust from motor vehicles. Hence a competitive cyclist should never ride flat out in urban areas, but rather in a restrained manner.

Cycling at high speed in a group requires great concentration. In the centre of this bunch is one of the most successful female racing cyclists, Ute Enzenauer.

Gear Ratios

The theory behind 'the ratio' is to develop your physical capabilities as much as is possible under ideal conditions and to adapt them to the varying types of terrain you will encounter. Wind conditions affect cycling a great deal, but cycling with the correct ratio enables you to adapt the variables of power, speed and endurance to the prevailing situation in the most economical way.

Ratio Measurements

In technical terms the word 'ratio' means the difference in size between the two gear cogs, and the number of times the mounting shafts of these cogs rotate in relation to each other.

When cycling, the ratio and input of pedal power depends upon the following factors:

1. The number of teeth on the front chainwheel.
2. The number of teeth on the freewheel.
3. The length of the cranks.
4. The diameter of the 'powered' wheel (the back wheel).

The diameter of the normal adult's bicycle wheel is 28 inches, while for a racing bicycle it is 27 inches. (The use of these imperial measurements can be traced back to the time of the original penny-farthing bicycles). However, the diameter of a racing-bicycle wheel nowadays is only 26.4 inches (which, in metric measurements is 26.4 x 2.54cm = 67.06cm) because of the thinner wheels. The circumference of a wheel like this is 209–211cm – depending upon the thickness of the tyres. Given this measurement, the ratio is now dependent only upon the size of the particular chainwheel in use and the respective cog of the freewheel, as the dimensions of the wheel and of the cranks are rarely variable.

There are a variety of different ways in which to determine the ratio of the respective gear positions. The following figures are necessary for this:

z_1 = The number of teeth on the chainwheel.
z_2 = The number of teeth on the freewheel.
d = The diameter of the rear wheel.
u = The circumference of the rear wheel.

There are actually four possible ways in which to indicate the ratio:

1. The actual ratio, that is the result of dividing the number of teeth on the chainwheel into the number of teeth on the freewheel.
2. The number in inches, that is the proportion of the number of teeth on the chainwheel and the freewheel compared with the rear wheel diameter.

Riding Skills

Gear table in inches*

No. of teeth on the cog	Chainwheel														
	38	40	42	44	45	46	48	49	50	51	52	53	54	55	56
12	83.28	87.67	92.05	96.43	98.63	100.82	105.20	107.39	109.58	111.78	113.97	116.16	118.35	120.54	122.73
13	76.88	80.92	84.97	89.02	91.04	93.06	97.11	99.13	101.15	103.18	105.20	107.22	109.25	111.27	113.29
14	71.39	75.14	78.90	82.66	84.54	86.41	90.17	92.05	93.93	95.81	97.69	99.56	101.44	103.32	105.20
15	66.63	70.13	73.64	77.15	78.90	80.65	84.16	85.91	87.67	89.42	91.17	92.93	94.68	96.43	98.19
16	62.46	65.75	69.04	72.33	73.97	75.61	78.90	80.54	82.19	83.83	85.48	87.12	88.76	90.41	92.05
17	58.79	61.88	64.98	68.07	69.62	71.16	74.26	75.81	77.35	78.90	80.45	81.99	83.54	85.09	86.64
18	55.52	58.44	61.37	64.29	65.75	67.21	70.13	71.59	73.06	74.52	75.98	77.44	78.90	80.36	81.82
19	52.60	55.37	58.14	60.91	62.29	63.67	66.44	67.83	69.21	70.59	71.98	73.36	74.75	76.13	77.52
20	49.97	52.60	55.23	57.86	59.18	60.49	63.12	64.44	65.75	67.07	68.38	69.70	71.01	72.33	73.64
21	47.59	50.10	52.60	55.10	56.36	57.61	60.11	61.37	62.62	63.87	65.12	66.38	67.63	68.88	70.13
22	45.43	47.82	50.21	52.60	53.80	54.99	57.38	58.58	59.77	60.97	62.16	63.36	64.55	65.75	66.95
23	43.45	45.74	48.03	50.31	51.46	52.60	54.89	56.03	57.17	58.32	59.46	60.60	61.75	62.89	64.03
24	41.64	43.83	46.03	48.22	49.31	50.41	52.60	53.70	54.79	55.89	56.98	58.08	59.18	60.27	61.37
25	39.98	42.08	44.18	46.29	47.34	48.39	50.50	51.55	52.60	53.65	54.70	55.76	56.81	57.86	58.91
26	38.44	40.46	42.48	44.51	45.52	46.53	48.55	49.57	50.58	51.59	52.60	53.61	54.62	55.63	56.65
27	37.01	38.96	40.91	42.86	43.83	44.81	46.76	47.73	48.70	49.68	50.65	51.63	52.60	53.57	54.55
28	35.69	37.57	39.45	41.33	42.27	43.21	45.09	46.03	46.96	47.90	48.84	49.78	50.72	51.66	52.60
29	34.46	36.28	38.09	39.90	40.81	41.72	43.53	44.44	45.34	46.25	47.16	48.07	48.97	49.88	50.79
30	33.31	35.07	36.82	38.57	39.45	40.33	42.08	42.96	43.83	44.71	45.59	46.46	47.34	48.22	49.09

* These measurements are based upon a wheel of a racing bicycle with a diameter of 26.3 inches.

3. The number of metres covered by one pedal revolution.

4. The number of teeth on the freewheel and on the chainwheel.

The Actual Ratio

This can be determined by dividing the number of teeth on the chainwheel by the number of teeth on a particular cog, for example 52/13 = 4/1, or 42/14 = 3/1. This simple ratio is, however, used very rarely.

Ratio in Inches

This measurement is often used by professional cyclists and is found by using the following formula:

$$\text{Ratio (in inches)} = \frac{z_1 \times d}{z_2}$$

The diameter of the rear wheel is measured in inches (and is usually 27 inches). For example: suppose there are 42 teeth on the chainwheel in the front, 16 teeth on the cog of the freewheel with a 27-inch diameter wheel:

$$\frac{42 \times 27}{16} = 70.88 \text{ inches}$$

As already mentioned, the diameter of today's racing-bicycle wheels is only about 26.4 inches (because of the thin tyres) – this also applies to training tyres. In fact, you are only left with a diameter of 26.3 inches on average once you have taken the dent (caused by the extra weight during cycling) into consideration. The following tables are based on this modern and very precise foundation. This means that the ratio of the previous example would actually be worked out as follows:

$$\frac{42 \times 26.3}{16} = 69.04 \text{ inches}$$

Ratio in Metres

Another indirect measurement of the ratio is the distance covered by one revolution of the pedal. This measurement is dependent both upon the circumference of the wheel and the ratio between the number of teeth on the chainwheel and on the freewheel. The relationship between the diameter and the circumference of a circle is π (= 3.1415926535 ... rounded down to 3.14) and so the formula for the circumference (u) is:

$$u = d \times \pi$$

This means that the circumference of a rear wheel with a diameter of 27 inches is:

The distance covered by one pedal revolution in different gears. The difference becomes increasingly smaller as the number of teeth on the cog increases. This is why a greater difference in the number of teeth must be chosen for an even staggering of gears.

$$u = 27 \times 2.54cm \times 3.14 = 215.3cm$$

But time has passed . . . and the wheels of today's racing bicycles have, because of their narrow and low tyres, an average circumference of only 209–211cm. The measurements in this book refer to a rear wheel with an average circumference of 210cm.

The measurement for the ratio in metres is determined by using the following formula:

$$\text{Ratio (m)} = \frac{z_1 \times u}{z_2}$$

Gear table in metres*

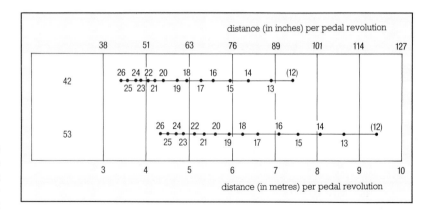

For example, the ratio of 42/16 corresponds to the following distance for each pedal revolution:

$$\frac{42}{16} \times 2.10m = 5.51m$$

A ratio of 69 inches corresponds to 5.51m per pedal revolution.

Ratio by Number of Teeth

The ratio is usually given in inches, but sometimes simply by the number of teeth. Cyclists in countries such as France and Italy prefer to quote the ratio in metres covered by one pedal revolution. It is perhaps easier for us to grasp the difference between the two

No. of teeth on the cog	Chainwheel														
	38	40	42	44	45	46	48	49	50	51	52	53	54	55	56
12	6.65	7.00	7.35	7.70	7.88	8.05	8.40	8.58	8.75	8.93	9.10	9.28	9.45	9.63	9.80
13	6.14	6.46	6.78	7.11	7.27	7.43	7.75	7.92	8.08	8.24	8.40	8.56	8.72	8.88	9.05
14	5.70	6.00	6.30	6.60	6.75	6.90	7.20	7.35	7.50	7.65	7.80	7.95	8.10	8.25	8.40
15	5.32	5.60	5.88	6.16	6.30	6.44	6.72	6.86	7.00	7.14	7.28	7.42	7.56	7.70	7.84
16	4.99	5.25	5.51	5.78	5.91	6.04	6.30	6.43	6.56	6.69	6.83	6.96	7.09	7.22	7.35
17	4.69	4.94	5.19	5.44	5.56	5.68	5.93	6.05	6.18	6.30	6.42	6.55	6.67	6.79	6.92
18	4.43	4.67	4.90	5.13	5.25	5.37	5.60	5.72	5.83	5.95	6.07	6.18	6.30	6.42	6.53
19	4.20	4.42	4.64	4.86	4.97	5.08	5.31	5.42	5.53	5.64	5.75	5.86	5.97	6.08	6.19
20	3.99	4.20	4.41	4.62	4.73	4.83	5.04	5.15	5.25	5.36	5.46	5.57	5.67	5.78	5.88
21	3.80	4.00	4.20	4.40	4.50	4.60	4.80	4.90	5.00	5.10	5.20	5.30	5.40	5.50	5.60
22	3.63	3.82	4.01	4.20	4.30	4.39	4.58	4.68	4.77	4.87	4.96	5.06	5.15	5.25	5.35
23	3.47	3.65	3.83	4.02	4.11	4.20	4.38	4.47	4.57	4.66	4.75	4.84	4.93	5.02	5.11
24	3.33	3.50	3.68	3.85	3.94	4.03	4.20	4.29	4.38	4.46	4.55	4.64	4.73	4.81	4.90
25	3.19	3.36	3.53	3.70	3.78	3.86	4.03	4.12	4.20	4.28	4.37	4.45	4.54	4.62	4.70
26	3.07	3.23	3.39	3.55	3.63	3.72	3.88	3.96	4.04	4.12	4.20	4.28	4.36	4.44	4.52
27	2.96	3.11	3.27	3.42	3.50	3.58	3.73	3.81	3.89	3.97	4.04	4.12	4.20	4.28	4.36
28	2.85	3.00	3.15	3.30	3.38	3.45	3.60	3.68	3.75	3.83	3.90	3.98	4.05	4.13	4.20
29	2.75	2.90	3.04	3.19	3.26	3.33	3.48	3.55	3.62	3.69	3.77	3.84	3.91	3.98	4.06
30	2.66	2.80	2.94	3.08	3.15	3.22	3.36	3.43	3.50	3.57	3.64	3.71	3.78	3.85	3.92

* These measurements are based upon a wheel of a racing bicycle with a circumference of 210cm.

ratios of 87 inches (53/16) and 69 inches (42/16) rather than the difference between the two lengths of 6.96m and 5.51m. But in the end it is perhaps easiest for the user to recognise the ratio by the number of teeth, for example 53/16, 42/16 and so forth.

Ratio Tables

Ratio tables are available both in inches and in metres (for the distance covered by one pedal revolution) in order to avoid mathematical calculations every time a new freewheel is fitted. The tables in this book are based on the latest measurements available for modern racing bicycles with rear wheels of diameter 26.3 inches and circumference 210cm.

Standard Freewheels

Your experience as a cyclist should be used fully when constructing a freewheel. Only the four outer cogs of a six-speed freewheel are normally used with the large chainwheel and only the four inner cogs with the small chainwheel. The freewheel should be manufactured in such a way that a well-staggered ratio is possible under these conditions – and without repeating a ratio (51/17 is in fact the same as 42/14). The following standard arrangement has proved to be effective:

Chainwheels: 53 and 42 teeth.
Freewheel: 13, 14, 15, 17, 19 and 21 teeth.

The difference between the teeth has to increase towards the top if an effective staggering is to be achieved. The gears would be changed in the following order when changing up using this standard ratio:

42/21 (52.6 inch; 4.20m)
42/19 (58.1 inch; 4.64m)
42/17 (65.0 inch; 5.19m)
42/15 (73.6 inch; 5.88m)

53/19 (73.4 inch; 5.86m)
53/17 (82.0 inch; 6.55m)
53/15 (93.0 inch; 7.42m)
53/14 (99.6 inch; 7.95m)
53/13 (107.2 inch; 8.56m)

The ratios 53/19 and 42/15 are practically identical but the chain is not even in either case. Which gear is preferable depends upon your situation; you would change the gear to 53/19 if you decided to leave the chain on the large chainwheel. However, you would change the gear to 42/15 if the chain was already positioned around the small chainwheel and the terrain demanded the continued use of this chainwheel.

The following arrangement of chainwheels and cogs might be advisable in mountainous terrain:

Chainwheels: 53/42
Freewheels: 13, 14, 15, 17, 20, 24.

Cyclists who ride on mountain passes will need a larger freewheel of 26 or even 28 teeth.

During time trials special freewheels are used. The cogs of these freewheels are regularly staggered with a difference of one tooth in every cog, perhaps: 13, 14, 15, 16, 17, 18 or 12, 13, 14, 15, 16, 17. A time-trial freewheel is unsuitable for cycling in open country as the differences between gears are too small for normal usage.

The Different Qualities of Similar Ratios

There are sometimes a number of options in which you can vary the number of teeth in the chainwheel and in the cog – and still be left with the same ratio (as shown in the ratio tables). The ratio 53/19, for instance, is almost identical to the ratio 42/15 (they are both about 74 inches) – and also to other ratios such as 56/20, 50/18, 45/16 and 39/14. Although these ratios are all practically the same from a purely quantitative point of view, they are,

however, different from a qualitative point of view – so that it does matter which ratio you choose.

The ratio with the largest total number of teeth, that is the larger chainwheel used with the larger cog, has the following advantages over the other possible permutations for the same ratio:

1.   Better distribution of power over a larger number of teeth.
2.   A decrease in tangential powers of the chain, freewheel and rear hub.
3.   A decrease in torsional powers affecting the frame.
4.   Smooth, round pedal revolutions.

These, however, should be weighed against the following disadvantages:

1.   A longer chain may be necessary.
2.   The system which transmits power weighs more.
3.   A decrease in propelling power; the system is softer.

The contrasting advantages and disadvantages apply to ratios with a small total number of teeth. Ideally, you should choose the ratio with the largest total number of teeth for time trialling and for longer stretches on flat ground.

The smaller total number of teeth with a harder, more agile ratio is usually preferred when riding in hilly terrain and in races where fast sprints and fast speed changes are required. This discussion clearly demonstrates how intricate judgements can be within cycling. A practical example of this is the ratio of 89 inches used in track cycling; the number of teeth used for track pursuit, which is ridden at a constantly high speed is 51/15. However, the number of teeth used for a track sprint, in which the propelling speed at the start of the race is absolutely vital, is a harder system of 48/14 teeth.

The Optimal Speed for a Pedal Revolution

This is one of the most interesting aspects of the sport because both the experience of generations of cyclists and scientific findings are interwoven.

Cyclists have always preferred a high frequency of pedal revolutions because they believed that this was the only way for them to reach top form. Indeed, the following rule can be formulated: the fitter cyclist prefers a high pedal frequency at a certain speed while the cyclist whose performance is on the decline seeks refuge in the lower pedalling frequency with higher gears at the same speed. This seems to support scientific research into pedalling frequency which indicates that low pedalling frequencies are more economical. The strong cyclist seems to waste his extra energy by cycling with a high pedalling frequency while the weaker cyclist uses his energy more sparingly. However, there is another rule which refutes this: the performance of cyclists who ride in too high a gear with too low a pedalling frequency too soon and too long decreases – and they will lose their fitness.

These two rules are of great practical importance to every cyclist and can be explained through modern tests on the composition and structure of muscle fibre. Two conclusions can be drawn from the simple formula, work = power × distance:

1. If the distance (that is the number of revolutions of the pedals) has decreased but you still do the same amount of work, it must follow that the power has increased.
2. If the input of power is decreased while still performing the same amount of work, the distance must then be increased – in other words, a larger number of pedal revolutions.

Riding Skills

Endurance cyclists should avoid the development of 'power fibres' in their muscles through too high a power input because they predominantly need 'endurance fibres' in their leg muscles in order to ward off fatigue and to have a large 'oxygen capacity'. Power fibres tire quickly and do not possess an oxygen capacity as large as that of endurance fibres and so fitness is lost. Endurance training must be undertaken in order to develop endurance fibres – and you should also avoid too high a power input over a long period of time. You must, according to the formula, increase the distance in order to make do with a smaller input of power at the same speed.

In cycling, increasing the distance means to cycle in a lower gear and carry out more pedal revolutions. Endurance fibres have to be built up during training and so the input of power should be comparatively small and high pedalling frequencies should be used. The optimal pedalling speed lies somewhere between 100 and 120 pedal rotations per minute. Small ratios (for example 42/18, 42/17 and 42/16) should be used for this type of exercise. Cycle races, however, are usually ridden with a large input of power because of the high speeds reached in such events. Endurance fibres have only limited power qualities so that racing cyclists use comparatively high pedalling frequencies – usually 90–100 per minute, even in races. It is also much easier to adjust to the different speeds required in a race when cycling at high pedalling frequencies.

There is one further advantage in cycling with high pedalling frequencies, namely improved blood circulation in your muscles. Circulation is hindered by muscle tension because the small blood vessels are squeezed together. The arterial blood supply is already noticeably decreased when twenty per cent of maximum power is used and the blood vessels are completely closed when fifty per cent of the maximum isometric contraction power is used. In other words, a large input of power hinders the blood circulation while relaxation of the muscles promotes it. The large power input during pedalling should also, for these reasons, be short and infrequent if possible so that the phases when the muscles are relaxed (and with a good supply of blood) occur more often. This is best achieved with a high pedalling frequency.

In principle, cyclists need to work with higher pedal ratios during training in order to achieve the optimal tuning of their bodies. During training a racing cyclist must be able to cycle with a high pedalling frequency over long distances without growing tired because speeds during a race will be much higher. In a race, though, speed changes all the time according to the tactics demanded – which means that it is not always possible (or desirable) to cycle in a high gear such as 53/13. Indeed the change of speed is usually effected by a change in pedalling frequency. After a race, particularly one ridden mainly in high gears, it is important to undertake training rides utilising low gears and high pedal frequencies; this is the only way to maintain your good condition.

A cyclist who always trains in high gears may become the 'training world champion' – but he or she will never reach their maximum capacity in races. Training and races require different ratios and different pedalling frequencies. Pedalling frequencies and the round pedalling action in cycling are sciences in themselves; they require patient and repeated practice. Only when you can master the optimal course of movements can you claim to be a cyclist.

Limiting Ratios for the Young

Cyclists are endurance athletes, and not power athletes. As the information given above shows, endurance in cycling is best developed by cycling at a high pedalling frequency. Endurance and power are two distinct qualities which compete with one another – by and large the development of power hinders the development of endurance. Therefore it is only logical to limit the ratio for young cyclists when they are developing and growing. If we follow the German National Cycling Federation, male and female cyclists can be graded according to age as follows:

Children, group C: 8–10 years
Children, group B: 10–12 years
Children, group A: 12–14 years
Juniors, group B: 14–16 years
Juniors, group A: 16–18 years
Amateurs: 18–35 years
Junior girls: 10–14 years
Girls: 14–18 years
Ladies: 18 years and over
Veterans: 35 years and over

The ratio limits, according once again to the German National Cycling Federation are based upon a wheel of diameter 27 inches and are as follows:

Children, groups B and C:
69 inches (for example 46/18 teeth)
Children, group A:
73.89 inches (for example 49/18 teeth)
Juniors, group B:
82.6 inches (for instance 52/17 teeth)

In the case of 'girls-only' races:

Girls aged 11–14: 69 inches
Girls aged 15–18: 82.6 inches

Young cyclists should learn to cycle in low gears with a high pedalling frequency from the beginning. This advice is based on the experience of several generations of cyclists – and is now supported by scientific research into the structure of muscle fibres. This is why you should ensure that a bicycle is not purchased for a child or youth with a ratio exceeding the limit for his or her age group – even if the child does not wish to become a racing cyclist. This is the only way for a child to develop endurance qualities which are both healthy and desirable.

Cycle training covers a huge area and it means different things to different people – according to how important cycling is to that particular individual. Ground rules for competitive sports apply in principle, as do those for popular and health-related sports – though not quite so markedly. Hence it is both important and interesting for cyclists, whichever category they may fit into,

to discover how they can achieve the best possible result with the least possible effort. You can always make great adjustments and significant progress simply through a sensible and intelligently planned and composed training programme – but especially in cycling.

The spring preparation period (here on Mallorca) promotes a relaxed, round pedal-action and strengthens fundamental endurance.

Ground Rules for Increasing Performance

The physical abilities of the human body tend to diminish if no exercise is taken. However, they adapt when the demands made upon them are increased so long as certain conditions are fulfilled. The following connections exist between capacity, adaptation and increased performance.

Training

Training Intensity and Training Quantity

Training must be of a certain intensity and quantity in order to trigger off adaptation processes. This is only possible if the exercise you take has a sufficient draw upon your physical reserves so that the training actually feels like an effort.

The exercise may be gentle in a modest training situation, but must increase as the training situation increases so that the process of adaptation – which will improve your performance – is promoted. This is why modest training is sufficient for popular and health-related sports while the quantity and intensity of training needed for competitive sports are sometimes almost inconceivable.

The Cycle of Supercompensation

Exertion, fatigue, recuperation and overcompensation (or supercompen-

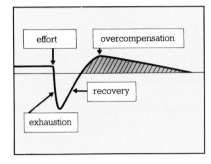

Cycle of overcompensation: regular alteration between exertion, fatigue, recuperation and overcompensation as the basis for the training process.

sation) are all interrelated phases within the training cycle. Every action which makes up effective training leads to a brief tiredness and a brief decrease in performance. The physiological adaptations which cyclists aim for occur during the process of 'rebuilding' of tissue, which 'regenerates' itself beyond its previous level – a phenomenon which is known as overcompensation or supercompensation. The theory is that as the tissue overcompensates for the work it has carried out, so it is better equipped to cope with

new and heavier loads. This phenomenon of a training stimulus promoting tissue growth through supercompensation is the basis for every improvement in performance. This is why exertion, fatigue, recuperation and overcompensation should be regarded as a single unit within training.

Performance Improvement

Every action which is effective training always has a result. There are, however, frequently periods in training during which there seems to be little or no improvement in performance, but what seems to be a standstill will, quite suddenly, turn out to be a large increase in performance at a later date – also known as a 'late transformation'. This phenomenon can sometimes be caused by very intensive training or hard races.

Training Situation and Quantity

Improvement in performance which is the result of training will diminish if the training which follows is not of the correct quality and frequency. An optimal increase of performance can only be achieved when the new training stimulus (or exercise) falls into the same pattern of supercompensation as the previous stimulus. There are, however, exercises designed to promote 'regeneration' or revitalisation, bringing about speedy recovery by way of an active recuperation. As the training intensity increases, so does the speed of recovery. This is why exertion can be accommodated with ever increasing frequency. If training is infrequent the time for recuperation will need to be longer. The optimisation of this process is very difficult.

The situation known as 'being in training' is not an irreversible process,

Summary of training effects. The benefits from overcompensation begin to decrease within 2–4 days in the case of infrequent training sessions (a). The increase in the build-up of performance is greater when the training uses larger and more frequent training stimuli (b). The maximum effect of training occurs when the new training load immediately follows the climax of overcompensation.

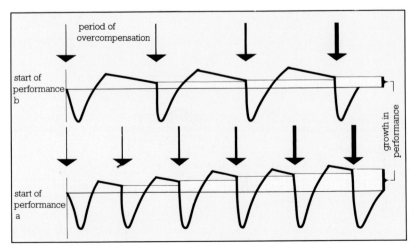

however, but a delicate equilibrium which constantly needs renewing; the body will always adapt to the active demands made upon it.

The following factors should always be kept in mind when planning training loads:

1. The intensity of the load.
2. The density of the load.
3. The quantity of the load.
4. The endurance of the load.
5. The structure of the load.
6. The degree of the load.
7. The frequency of the load.

The Profile of a Competitive Cyclist

It is sufficient to improve the basic endurance capacity through a training programme of low intensity, medium to large quantity and high pedalling speed at a minimum input of power. Leisure cyclists will also be able to understand better the adaptation process of their own training if they are aware of training programmes for competitive and highly competitive sports. The factors which determine performance from a racing cyclist's point of view are as follows:

1. Personal ability (character, willpower, motivation, intellectual abilities).
2. Fitness abilities (endurance, speed, power, suppleness).
3. Technique.
4. Tactics.

Every discipline within cycling has its own separate set of demands, particularly the fitness abilities of endurance, speed and power.

Rolf Golz, a favourite with German cycle fans, at a mountain finish during the Tour de Suisse.

Training

Psychological Foundations of Cycle Training

An important principle of training is that of 'consciousness'; the entire training should consciously be geared towards a particular goal. You should always understand which tasks you should set yourself, why they should be set and how – which will depend upon what you hope to achieve. This is the only way to control your own training. Extensive self-control is a prerequisite for an optimal control of training load.

The 'Human Machine'

Bicycle and cyclist are, of course, two different machines which ideally should operate in harmony. The two mechanisms are made from differing substances; one of metal, rubber and leather, the other of cells, tissue, organs and 'organ-systems'. Two machines – which are so different – can only co-operate economically when one is familiar with both. Cyclists should therefore be as familiar with the workings of their own body as with the technological operations of their bicycle, whatever type of machine it may be.

The construction and function of the human body can only be discussed briefly here. Cyclists should, however, learn about this from other sources in order to make significant progress.

A number of different, specialised organ-systems work together in the 'human machine':

1. The skeletal system (bones, joints, ligaments).
2. The muscle system (muscles, tendons).
3. The nervous system (the brain, nerves).
4. The vascular system (blood-vessels, lymph vessels).
5. The cardiorespiratory system (heart, lungs).
6. The digestive system (oesophagus, stomach, intestines, liver, pancreas).
7. The system of the endocrine glands (pituitary gland, thyroid gland, adrenal glands, gonads and pancreas).
8. The urinary system (kidneys, ureter, urethra, bladder).
9. The skin system (skin, hair, nails, sebaceous glands, sweat-glands).
10. The sensory system (eyes, ears, nose, touch, taste).

Life can be reduced, essentially, to movement, development of energy, and breathing with the inhalation of oxygen and exhalation of carbon dioxide.

Types of Energy Supply

The relationship between energy and biological structures – how it is stored and released – remains something of a mystery. The facts that energy can be stored in our body in the form of energy-rich phosphate bonds, and that it can be released when necessary are well known. These energy-rich phosphate bonds have to be reloaded through our metabolism so that there is always a sufficient supply of energy for the muscle movements, the functioning of organs and all the various other processes which need energy. Altogether there are three ways to release energy; which one is used largely depends upon the duration and intensity of the load.

A short, sharp exertion lasting 6–8 seconds. This may occur during a sprint of 60–80m and does not allow the cells opportunity to supply energy by way of the slow metabolic processes. The stored mass of energy, formed from energy-rich phosphate bonds and which is present in the working muscles themselves will release energy in this situation. There is not enough time, however, to transport sufficient oxygen to the muscles and so the energy is

Types of energy supply. 1 Energy supply from energy-rich phosphates (ATP, KP using anaerobic-alactic energy formation) during short, sharp loads. 2 The anaerobic energy formation of glycogen with the formation of lactic acid (anaerobic-lactic energy formation) during short and intensive performances (as needed when interval-training), duration 40–60 seconds. 3 Increasingly aerobic energy formation (of glycogen and/or fatty acids, according to the intensity of the load) used when the duration of the performance is increased (long-term intervals, long-term endurance) – in excess of two minutes.

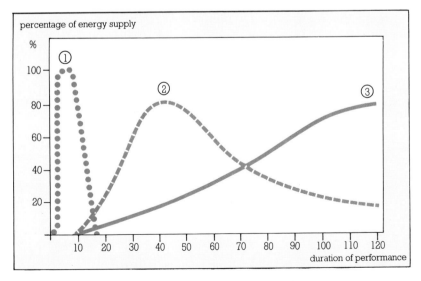

produced without oxygen (anaerobic respiration) and without the formation of lactic acid. This kind of energy production is consequently known as anaerobic–alactic energy formation.

Maximum performance lasting 40–50 seconds. Once again it is impossible to transmit sufficient oxygen during this kind of load (anaerobic respiration). The energy-rich phosphates which are stored in the muscles can only produce energy for a duration of 6–8 seconds. These energy-rich phosphates must quickly be regenerated by the use of glycogen (a supply of carbohydrate) or glucose (blood sugar). This respiration process results in the formation of lactic acid, which initially cannot be released without a supply of oxygen and so collects in the blood This form of energy production is therefore known as anaerobic–lactate energy formation. The action of the muscles becomes impeded when the acid in the blood has reached a certain level and the speed will have to be reduced. This is the most common form of energy formation in cycle sprints of 400–600m.

Exertion of two minutes or more. Such energy demands cannot be met without oxygen. In other words, the system needs oxygen in order to function (aerobic respiration). Cycling speeds are lower using this type of respiration, although they are maintainable for longer periods. After this process, the regeneration of energy-rich phosphate bonds is achieved by the oxidation of carbohydrates and fats. The rate and proportion at which carbohydrates and fats are broken down depends upon the type (endurance or power) and intensity of training. The optimising of the energy metabolism is the fundamental adaptation within cycle training.

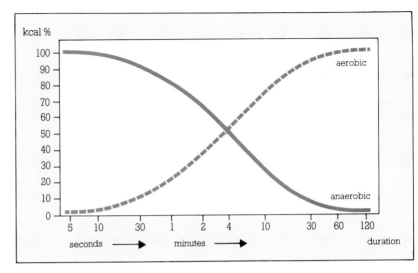

The percentages of aerobic and anaerobic capacity during maximum performances of different duration. Aerobic respiration (aerobic capacity) becomes the decisive factor during performances lasting longer than two minutes.

The Physiological Effect of Cycling

When we undertake cycling training our body undergoes certain changes which are called adaptations. The word adaptation in this context means, generally speaking, a change of physical or mental functional systems to a higher level of performance and also adjustment to particular external conditions, which occur because of the extent of physical exercise and training. Indeed, training loads result in functional, biochemical and structural changes and help improve psychological abilities. In principle, processes of adaptation can only come about when the training load corresponds to the optimal intensity for the body's capacity at any one moment – there is, of course, also a minimum quantity required before adaptation can occur. The type of adaptation depends upon the previous training load. Of the fitness components of power, speed and endurance, the latter is the most important for cyclists.

Endurance means, quite simply, the ability to carry out exercise over a long period of time without growing tired. There are two different stages in adaptation, differing only slightly from one another. Training for popular and health-related sports is generally of short duration and low intensity so that more functional improvements of the organ systems are developed. The basic endurance is the foundation for further increases in performance. The second, higher level of adaptation – for highly competitive sports – is achieved through training of high intensity and long duration. Only at this stage do organs such as the heart significantly increase their capacity. This specific competition endurance is a highly intensive endurance and must be based on the 'fundamental endurance'. The adaptation processes will be briefly described in the following pages.

The Effect of Cycling on the Heart and Circulation

Muscles require oxygen in order to create energy and so the body must ensure that enough oxygen is transported to the muscle cells. This process is improved by a better blood supply to the working muscles and by the development of new, small blood vessels (capillaries), as well as by a more efficient function of the heart and lungs – which provide the peripheral working muscles with oxygen and nourishment.

The requirements of these muscles are not particularly great in popular and health-related sports – which largely result in the development of fundamental endurance only – so that there is no necessity for the size of the heart to increase. A larger heart (the result of strenuous training) is, in other words, unlikely to be present in participants of popular or health-related sports. At best such a sportsperson will increase the amount of the stroke volume (the amount of blood pumped out from the heart at every beat), but there will be no external increase in the size of the heart. A person's breathing capacity will also be improved from this level of training. Generally speaking only at a higher intensity of training, such as for highly competitive sports with longer duration of training, is the volume of the heart enlarged. This increase (or adaptation) happens as a direct consequence of the increased need for oxygen in the working muscles. Hence athletes with the largest and most intensive endurance capacity possess hearts with the greatest volume – in simple terms.

It should be appreciated that the 'sports heart' is superior to the normal heart in several ways: it has adapted to the required performance and is neither weak nor inferior in any way; every muscle of the heart has become stronger through a demand for a greater supply of blood – a harmonious growth affecting every part of the heart. To meet this demand, the heart is accordingly better supplied with both blood and blood-vessels as the muscle fibres of the heart grow longer and thicker. This is how a further increase in the volume of the heartbeat is developed – so that a healthy, fit heart belonging to a sportsperson beats less frequently than that of an unfit office worker when both are doing similar

amounts of work. In fact, the daily work of a trained heart equals roughly half that of an untrained heart.

In spite of intensive training loads the heart is actually spared work in the long run. This means a marked decrease in the incidence of fatal coronary heart disease amongst people actively involved in popular and health-related sports, as compared with the 'normal' population. The resting pulse is a relatively good method of measuring the level of fitness. It is best to take your pulse in the morning before getting up. The pulse-rate of untrained people is usually 70–80 per minute. The pulse-rate of people actively involved in popular and health-related sports may fall to around 60 per minute or less; this decrease is possible through a relaxation of the autonomic nervous system – the body can thus make do with fewer heart beats without increasing the capacity of the heart. The resting pulse is even lower for an enlarged heart of a competitive cyclist; this averages about 40–50 beats per minute. The best pulse the author has come across was 28 beats per minute! A resting pulse which exceeds its normal level can be an early indication of illness or of excessive training.

The Effect of Cycling on the Nervous System

The nervous system is divided into two areas; the voluntary and involuntary (autonomic). The former consists of the brain, the spinal cord and the peripheral nerves. The latter, the involuntary – autonomic – nervous system is subdivided into the sympathetic and parasympathetic nervous systems which between them control the actions of the various organs and the entire sensory perceptions of the body. The functioning of the entire nervous system improves from endurance training. A shift of control takes place from the sympathetic to the parasympathetic in the autonomic nervous system. The athlete in training becomes calmer and is able to recuperate more

quickly. The psycho-physical capacity improves at the same rate as this ability to recover quickly. The change to the parasympathetic nervous system also results in a decrease in the resting pulse rate.

Maximum Oxygen Uptake (aerobic capacity)

The maximum oxygen uptake determines the upper limit for the intensity of exercise – that is it limits the speed which a cyclist can maintain over a long period without suffering from lack of oxygen. The volume of this maximum oxygen uptake is subject to a biological ageing process. A man of 20–30 years can inhale 3.3l of oxygen per minute, a woman of the same age around 2.2l. This means that these men and women breathe in 35–45ml of oxygen per kilogram of body-weight.

As your age increases, so this value decreases – and at the age of 70 is only around half its initial value. The majority of people simply accept this ageing process out of ignorance and see this degeneration as inevitable. These people should be told that it is quite possible to maintain your breathing capacity over many decades – and even increase it through an appropriate type of endurance training such as cycling. Highly trained endurance athletes achieve a breathing capacity of 6l per minute, that is around 80–90ml of oxygen per kilogram of body-weight! Cycle 'veterans' are most certainly able to build up and maintain a breathing capacity of 3l per minute and more, even up to the age of 60 or 70 years – almost corresponding to the value of an untrained 30-year-old! Cycling therefore makes it possible to remain 30 years old for a duration of 30 or 40 years – biologically, anyway – with the right kind of training.

Training

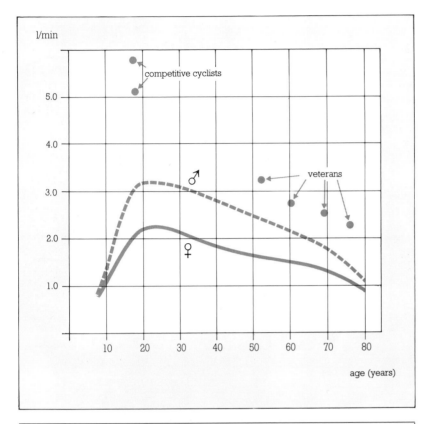

The maximum oxygen uptake at different ages for men and women in litres per minute. Values for individual competitive cyclists and veterans in endurance sports are shown for comparison.

This improved oxygen uptake is the result of the matabolism's adaptation to the training process and is, in turn, the result of a change within the composition of the muscle fibres of the working muscles.

Adaptation of the Metabolism

Aerobic metabolism processes (that is the formation of energy with oxygen) occur almost exclusively from the oxidation of carbohydrates and fats. Carbohydrates are stored in the muscles and liver in the form of glycogen. This glycogen consists of groups of chains of glucose molecules. These are separated and used in respiration when necessary.

The chemical formula for glucose is $C_6H_{12}O_6$ (C=carbon, H=hyrdrogen, O=oxygen) which means that one molecule of glucose carries six oxygen atoms. For the body this means that it needs additional nutrients which carry oxygen (carbohydrates or carbohydrate stores, such as glycogen) when the strain on the body is increased to such an extent that it has to function at the upper limit of oxygen uptake. Fats, on the other hand, carry comparatively very little oxygen. They, however, have a different advantage; they are able to store twice as much energy per unit of weight as the carbohydrates. The fat reserves of the body are also much larger than the glycogen reserves. This is why the glycogen stores are very valuable (but limited) sources of energy loads at the limit of maximum oxygen uptake, whereas more fats are used to generate energy during a less intensive load. In other

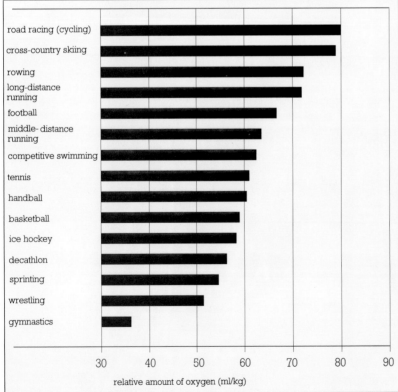

The maximum amounts of oxygen inhaled per kilogram of body-weight of selected competitive athletes from different disciplines.

words, the fat metabolism serves to spare the valuable carbohydrate reserves.

The fat metabolism, however, must be continually exercised so that the organism can utilise it as a form of energy. The fat metabolism is 'conditioned' by training for fundamental endurance (little or medium intensity and relatively high quality). The training should be carried out under optimal oxygen conditions so that the need for oxygen does not limit the conditioning of the fat metabolism. This is the most important form of training within popular and health-related sports. A well-developed fat metabolism is a biochemical sign of a body well developed for endurance training.

Every spring, professional cyclists train for this adaptation of the metabolism by covering long distances with a low ratio and low to average speed. The correct speed allows you to hold a conversation without becoming breathless. The cyclist's training must achieve two important aims:

1. To increase the maximum oxygen uptake.
2. To improve the generation of energy from fat metabolism.

These adaptations occur in the working muscles and result in the development of very special muscle fibres which fulfil both these aims.

Composition of Muscle Fibres

Biologists differentiate between various types of muscle fibre within a muscle. Two are of particular importance – the slow-twitch (ST) fibres and the fast-twitch (FT) fibres. The prerequisite for a high endurance ability is a large number of ST fibres which can be developed through appropriate training. You should familiarise yourself with the new findings about these fibres as they have a great impact on cycle training so far as the choice of ratio and the number of pedal revolutions are concerned.

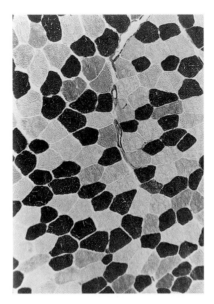 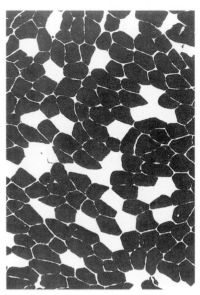

Muscle fibres and training. Left; about 50 per cent ST fibres before training. Right; about 80 per cent ST fibres after cycle training for six weeks (from research by H. Howald).

ST Fibres

Endurance training encourages muscle fibres with a high oxygen capacity which, in turn, demands a more effective aerobic energy metabolism. (The enzymes for the aerobic metabolism are present in the mitochondria, the 'power house' of the cell.) These muscle fibres are supplied with an increased amount of muscle colouring (myoglobin) which allows a better oxygen bond, so increasing the oxygen capacity. These fibres are surrounded by numerous little blood vessels (capillaries) for a better circulation. They also hold an increased amount of glycogen and fat as energy reserves. Their speed of contraction and their power ability are lower than for FT fibres but their resilience to fatigue is much higher. These fibres are also known as slow, red fibres (or muscle fibres of type 1) for the reasons mentioned above. ST fibres are thin and so can be supplied with oxygen much more easily than the thicker FT fibres.

FT Fibres

These muscle fibres are better equipped for anaerobic respiration (the generating of energy without oxygen). They hold fewer of the enzymes which promote aerobic respiration (that is fewer mitochondria), less muscle colouring (myoglobin) and fewer small blood vessels (capillaries). The energy reserves are left without oxygen in anaerobic respiration which means more energy rich phosphates – almost as much glycogen as in ST fibres – but no reserves of fat. Their speed of contraction is quicker and their power ability more extensive but their resilience to fatigue is reduced and so these fibres are also known as white, fast fibres (muscle fibres type 2). The protein structure and the cross-section of the FT fibres must be increased in order to cope with the power loads and so they are thicker than ST fibres – hence it is more difficult to supply them with oxygen.

Training

A comparison between ST and FT fibres.

	ST fibres	FT fibres
fibre thickness	thin	thick
maximum amount of oxygen	high	low
muscle colouring (myoglobin) for oxygen transport	high	low
enzymes used in aerobic metabolism (mitochondria)	numerous	few
the ability to form new blood-vessels (capillaries)	high	few
energy stores: energy-rich phosphates (ATP, KP) glycogen fats	low high high	high high low
anaerobic enzymes (formation of lactic acid)	low	high
development of power	low to medium	high
fatigue	low	high

1. ST fibres are improved by cycling over long distances in small gears and with a high number of pedal revolutions.

2. FT fibres are improved primarily by cycling short distances in high gears, with a large input of power and a small number of pedal revolutions. It has been claimed that too high a proportion of intensive, interval training with a large amount of aerobic respiration may promote the conversion of ST fibres into FT fibres.

3. ST fibres are thinner than FT fibres. Accordingly, thin legs are often a sign of good condition in cycling – while large legs tend to show a degeneration of a cyclist's condition. Generally speaking, thin legs are usually better so far as endurance is concerned be-

Muscle Fibres of the Intermediate Type

These muscle fibres, called intermediate fibres or fibres of type 2A, have a contraction ability and metabolism function which lies between those of the two other types of fibre. They can be turned into ST fibres or FT fibres according to demand.

ST fibres, Endurance Performance and Endurance Training

Scientific studies have shown that there is an equal ratio of ST to FT fibres in the majority of the population. Highly trained endurance athletes, however, show a proportion of up to 9:1 in favour of ST fibres. This corresponds exactly with the high endurance performance level of these athletes.

Tests seem to indicate that the intermediate fibres in particular can be turned into ST fibres through correct endurance training – but they will be turned into FT fibres if you train incorrectly. ST fibres soon degenerate during rest periods, for instance after an injury or when training frequency diminishes.

The Consequences of the Training Process

The type of training load and its frequency determine the composition of the muscle fibre structure in the long run – and this forms the foundation for the desired level of performance. The heart, circulatory and respiratory systems then adapt to these adjustments in order to supply the developed performance structure with sufficient oxygen and nourishment.

Optimal Training Loads

Endurance and power, by and large, compete with one another and should be of a particular ratio within competitive cycling. Cyclists should, initially, build up ST fibres in their muscles by embarking upon endurance training – that is they should cycle long distances with little power input. The ratio of endurance to power is determined by the utilisation of the appropriate gears – this is totally different from other sports disciplines. The following fundamental rules can be deduced from today's knowledge of the training process within cycling:

cause thin muscle fibres can be better supplied with oxygen whereas big legs tire easily and are more likely to suffer from oxygen deficiency.

4. Training with a high number of pedal revolutions and small input of power using low gears should always follow events which were ridden with high gears and a low number of pedal revolutions in order to prevent the development of FT fibres and promote the redevelopment of ST fibres.

5. In order to maintain the developed ST fibres, you should train at least three or four times every week.

Cross-country races require endurance, technique and athleticism – here shown by Dieter Uebing, who, at over 40 years of age, is still one of the world's top cross-country cyclists.

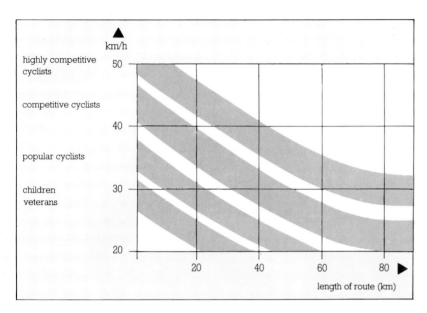

Areas of effective training (length of route and average speed) of cyclists at different levels of performance (adapted from H . Harre).

6. The training programme of a cyclist should be as much as 90 per cent endurance training. The proportion of speed and interval work should therefore be accordingly smaller – and should always be followed by relaxed endurance training.

The Amount of Training

The main requirements for increased performance and training control are intensity, duration (quantity) and frequency of the training load. Your current load requirement, your current capacity and your current endurance load all determine the amount of load to which you should subject your body through a particular training schedule. In other words, the less fit you are, the more you should guard against too intensive a training load because the beneficial effects of training decreases once a certain degree of fatigue is reached. There are, perhaps, four different stages of fatigue: little fatigue; medium fatigue; optimal fatigue; and strong fatigue. Good training

causes medium to strong fatigue. Cyclists should still be willing and able to work both mentally and physically after a training load of this level; you should feel fresh and should have recuperated by the following morning. You should be able to repeat the same type and amount of training 24 (or at most 48) hours after the preceding training. Put simply, the quantity of training should decrease when the intensity increases – and vice versa. The duration of training can increase if the intensity decreases. Junior and veteran cyclists should be particularly careful not to exceed a sensible amount of intensive training, as should cyclists in the popular and health-related sports section of cycling. Highly intensive training loads are really only to be recommended for active cyclists who aim to improve their personal best performance or who are training for a competition.

Intensity Levels and Training Control

Optimal training means achieving the best possible training effect over a relatively short period of time. The most

important factor is the choice of the right intensity – the ratio, the number of pedal revolutions and the speed. The majority of mistakes in this area are made by cyclists who participate for health or recreational reasons and who tend to cycle at too high an intensity (too fast). This is why it is very important to develop a good feeling for the optimal training intensity. There are, apart from fatigue (usually a good enough indication of the training load within recreational and health-related cycling), other means of determining the level of intensity for advanced professional cyclists and those actively involved in competitive cycling.

For this purpose the training is broken down into intensity levels so that each level can be combined with a particular aim to form a training programme. In this way the training process can always be adjusted to suit the individual's current performance. There are also some other fundamental rules which should be mentioned here. The body's need for oxygen increases in proportion to the level of intensity of performance. The maximum endurance capacity is reached when the maximum oxygen uptake ($\dot{V}O_2$max) – also called the aerobic capacity – has been used up.

The body suffers an oxygen deficit if this limit has been exceeded by a continued increase in the intensity of the load and energy has to be generated partially by anaerobic respiration (without oxygen). Lactic acid is developed as a by-product of this metabolism and its level increases with the intensity of the load. The concentration of lactic acid in the blood, the presence of which indicates that the border between aerobic and anaerobic respiration has been crossed, is called the anaerobic threshold.

This point is reached at a lactic acid level of 4mmol/l. Once this point has been reached the level rises quickly. The maximum oxygen uptake increases with an increased endurance capacity – and the anaerobic threshold (above which the level of lactic acid will rise quickly) occurs after a more intense level of performance. An individual's 'lactic performance curve' characterises the current level of performance and is used for training control in highly competitive sports. Its use, however, is not yet possible in popular and health-related cycling. Nevertheless, it is possible to recognise at which level of intensity you are through direct and indirect signs.

Your pulse rate can be used as a measurement which can help you control your training intensity without an exact knowledge of the anaerobic threshold (don't forget that the maximum heartbeat frequency declines with age). The optimal training pulse for popular and health-related sport is usually found by using the formula 180 minus your age. Further values can be seen in the table. Every cyclist who wishes to embark upon competitive cycling at or over the age of 35, should undergo a medical examination (which in turn should include the use of a bicycle ergometer). This device (see illustration on page 123) indicates your pulse at the different training load levels and so is very useful for training control.

You should learn by rote the following levels of intensity so that you always know at which level of intensity you are at any particular moment in your training.

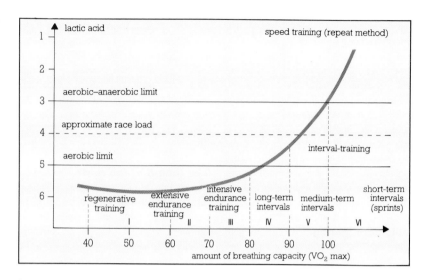

Levels of intensity and the lactic performance curve.

Intensity Level 1

The aim. At this level you aim for relaxed training for regeneration of muscle fibres, active recuperation, technique training and training to improve the metabolism of fat.

Intensity. The amount of load is low, approximately 40–60 per cent of the maximum oxygen uptake (maximum aerobic performance). When at this intensity level, it is quite possible to hold a conversation of several sentences without struggling for breath. Breathing, indeed, is calm and even, the pulse around 160 beats minus your age. Recreational cyclists will ride at around 15–20kmh and competitive cyclists about 25–28kmh, each using small gears such as 42/18.

Subjective feeling. You feel free and relaxed, you can enjoy the fresh air and your surroundings as well as appreciate the round pedal-movement. You are relaxed and have time to enjoy conversation and look at the countryside.

Length of the route. In popular and health-related cycling the length of the ride should be 20–40km; for competitive cyclists, this should be increased to 60–100km or more.

Intensity Level 2

The aim. The aim now is to achieve a fundamental endurance capacity and to improve the metabolism of fat involving endurance training with low intensity (extensive endurance training). Technique training should aim for a round pedal-action using a high frequency of

Training control; the relationship between training intensity (levels of intensity), maximum intake of oxygen (as a percentage) and the pulse when training – at different ages.

level of intensity	maximum intake of oxygen (as a percentage)	pulse when training (beats per minute minus your age)	examples at different ages				
			20yrs	30yrs	40yrs	50yrs	60yrs
			pulse				
I	40–60	160 – age	140	130	120	110	100
II	60–70	170 – age	150	140	130	120	110
III	70–80	180 – age	160	150	140	130	120
IV	80–90	190 – age	170	160	150	140	130
V	90–100	200 – age	180	170	160	150	
VI	100–120	210 – age	190	180	170		

Training _____

pedal revolutions (100–120rpm) and low gears such as 42/17.

Intensity. The amount of load is still low, around two-thirds of the maximum breathing capacity. Breathing is slightly faster but you can still easily manage a number of sentences without losing your breath. Your pulse will be about 170 beats minus your age. Recreational cyclists will ride at 20–25kmh while competitive cyclists will reach about 30kmh.

Subjective feeling. You are moving quite fast but the speed does not feel uncomfortable. You are still relaxed, can appreciate the surroundings and hold a conversation without any great difficulty. Breathing and heart beat are barely noticeable.

The length of the route. In popular and health-related cycling the length of the ride should be 30–40km; for competitive cyclists, this should be increased to 80–100km.

Intensity Level 3

The aim. This is intensive, aerobic endurance training which aims to improve aerobic metabolism giving rise to roughly equal proportions of fat and carbohydrate metabolism (muscular glycogen is also partially used). There is no noticeable formation of lactic acid. Ultimately, training at this level of intensity develops determination as well as the ability to cycle at speed.

Intensity. The amount of load is about 70–80 per cent of the maximum oxygen uptake. Breathing is now slightly increased but it is possible to utter short sentences without becoming breathless. The pulse is normally about 180 beats per minute minus your age. Recreational cyclists usually ride at around 30kmh and competitive cyclists at around 35–38 kmh, using low to medium gears such as 42/16 or 53/17.

Subjective feeling. This now feels as

though it is intensive training; your breathing will be a little increased but you should not be breathless. Concentration and determination are now necessary and your field of vision will be slightly narrower although you can still take in your surroundings. The desire for conversation decreases, however!

The length of the route. In popular and health-related cycling the length of the ride should be 20–30km; for competitive cyclists, this should be increased to 40–120km – or perhaps even further.

Important for recreational cyclists: you should not train more intensively than this level – indeed the majority of training should take place at levels 1 and 2. The following levels of intensity should be left to competitive cyclists only.

Intensity Level 4

The aim. Training at this level of intensity develops both determination and powerful speed. It also leads to power endurance with race speed. This form of training uses relatively high gears – but with a high number of revolutions, for example a ratio of 53/16 with 90–100 pedal revolutions per minute. The system of energy metabolism is still aerobic, with the lactic-acid level around the anaerobic threshold. At this level of intensity, carbohydrate is predominantly metabolised as well as muscle glycogen.

Intensity. The amount of load is 80–90 per cent of the maximum oxygen capacity. It is only possible to maintain this intensity over a long period of time if you are very fit. Breathing is noticeably faster and it is only possible to speak a few, short words. The pulse is about 190 beats minus your age.

Subjective feeling. Rapid breathing and the beginning of lactic acid production convey the feeling of a heavier load. The field of vision is narrower and

limited to the winding of the road and the countryside at the immediate roadside. Increased will-power and concentration are necessary for this kind of training.

The length of the route. This intensive training should be avoided by recreational cyclists or those who cycle for health reasons (apart from the occasional interval-training of 1–2 minutes). This is the level of intensity for longer bursts of interval-training for competitive cyclists, for instance during the spring training programme within a group (changing every 2–4 minutes) or during intervals of 5–10 minutes or more during solo training rides.

Intensity Level 5

The aim. The aim of this is anaerobic training with an increase in the level of lactic acid above the anaerobic threshold. It increases power and speed endurance for interval-training of a medium duration (2–10 minutes); it is useful for familiarisation to race speed and for developing the power needed to break away from a group. Power endurance training is practised by cycling in high gears (for instance 53/15) with a high number of pedal revolutions – about 90–100 per minute.

Intensity. The amount of load is by now about 90–100 per cent of the maximum oxygen uptake or slightly more. Breathing is considerably faster and you can only utter fractions of words with gasps for breath between them. The pulse is about 200 beats a minute minus your age. Your speed is slightly faster than race speed.

Subjective feeling. The rising level of lactic acid causes a feeling of reluctance. Your field of vision and thought are considerably narrowed and you are only aware of the roadside and the winding of the road. Will-power and concentration are of vital importance.

The length of the route. This should be of medium duration; 2–10 minutes during interval training and 1–2 minutes when leading a group.

Intensity Level 6

The aim. This level of intensity is for training for power, sprint ability, and for speed and power endurance. The system of energy metabolism is now more anaerobic and the level of lactic acid increases in proportion to the duration of the load.

Intensity. The amount of load is now about 100–120 per cent of the maximum breathing capacity, exceeding the limit of the aerobic capacity and so resulting in oxygen deficiency and formation of lactic acid. The 'limit' of breathing is reached and it is impossible to talk. Your pulse is about 210 beats minus your age and your speed is considerably faster than race speed. Speeds and pedal revolutions are both high – or alternatively a lower speed using small to medium gears with a very high number of pedal revolutions (over 130 per minute).

Subjective feeling. Maximum will-power is called for and this load is only possible with total motivation. A high level of lactic acid and breathlessness both result in a strong feeling of reluctance.

The length of the route. This should be 20–30 seconds when leading a group – perhaps during the 100km team race – during which time comparatively little lactic acid is formed both because of the short duration and because energy is generated anaerobically by energy-rich phosphates. There is a noticeable increase in the level of lactic acid during interval-training lasting 45–120 seconds, particularly during stage races or training. It is possible to improve (through training) both the efficiency of this anaerobic metabolism and the psychological tolerance of this level of intensity by:

1. Training and subsequent accumulation of the energy-rich phosphates (anaerobic non-lactic generation of energy) through short sprints of 10–30 seconds.
2. Training of the anaerobic-lactic formation of energy with a rise in the level of lactic acid through a load duration of 45–120 seconds.
3. Training to increase the tolerance of high levels of lactic acid within the blood.

Experience has shown that you should not train too frequently at intensity levels 5 and 6 because too much training these levels will, paradoxically, stagnate your level of performance – or even decrease it! In other words, the ability to ride at a high speed does not necessarily come about by constantly training at a high speed. An increase in performance is often only rediscovered once the training load has been reduced to stages 2 and 3!

The following principle is generally applicable: the shorter a training route is, the higher the level of intensity should be – and vice versa (the longer a training route is, the lower the level of intensity). The training load should not lead to complete exhaustion but to a medium level of fatigue – only occasionally should you become very tired.

Time trialling calls for endurance with immense intensity, concentration and will-power.

It is important to know that the levels of the stress hormones noradrenalin and adrenalin rise at almost the same rate as the level of lactic acid – and that the blood pressure rises with the hormones. This is why recreational cyclists should avoid these higher levels of intensity.

Competitive cyclists should use them, but only sparingly, and allow plenty of time for recovery or at least include an active period of training at levels 1 and 2. Junior cyclists, in particular, should invariably follow this principle because their autonomic nervous system requires more time to recuperate than that of a fully developed adult cyclist.

Endurance and Endurance Training

Endurance means the ability to carry out a particular exercise over a long period of time without becoming tired. The speed should be reached and then maintained through an optimal ratio between input of power and number of pedal revolutions. There are two different types of endurance within cycling:

1. Fundamental or basic endurance.
2. Racing-specific endurance: short-duration endurance, medium-duration endurance, long-duration endurance, power endurance, speed endurance.

These forms of endurance are interrelated. *Fundamental (or basic) endurance* forms the basis for all other forms of endurance; it allows the tolerance of intensive training loads and increases the ability to regenerate muscle fibres. It is achieved by training at low to medium intensity levels (cycling at about 20–30kmh) with a high number of pedal revolutions (100–120 per minute), a small input of power

(perhaps 42/17 or 42/18) and a long route (40–200km, depending upon the level of performance). This kind of training will develop ST fibres in the working muscles. Biochemically speaking, the fat metabolism is predominantly used. The muscles remain thin and are well supplied with blood and oxygen. All adaptations of intensity level 1 are reached.

Racing-specific endurance is marked by a higher intensity (speed 35–40kmh) as compared with fundamental endurance. Racing-specific endurance is achieved by riding in higher gears (for instance 53/16) with a higher number of pedal revolutions (90–100rpm) and a length of route roughly equivalent to – or longer than – that of a race. The intensity of the load is in the vicinity of the anaerobic threshold and approaches the limit of the oxygen uptake capacity. Additional carbohydrates, which have a larger oxygen store than fats, are used to generate energy. Training for fundamental endurance predominantly burns up fat stores, while training for racing-specific endurance makes great demands upon the carbohydrate metabolism.

Short-duration endurance (loads of 45–120 seconds) and *medium-duration endurance* (loads of 2–10 minutes) are abilities needed predominantly for track racing and so will not be discussed further here.

Long duration endurance is required for performances which last between 10 minutes and a number of hours as is common in road races. Performance is predominantly brought about through aerobic metabolism. Anaerobic metabolism with an oxygen deficiency is only used under certain tactical circumstances in road races – such as attempts to break away from a group, spurts during a race, climbing and the final sprint.

Power endurance means a high-power performance over a long period; this is called for on long rides, hill-stages, hill races and during time trials. Power-endurance training is undertaken by cycling with a large input

The interrelationship of power and speed during short-term, medium-term and long-term endurance (after D. Harre).

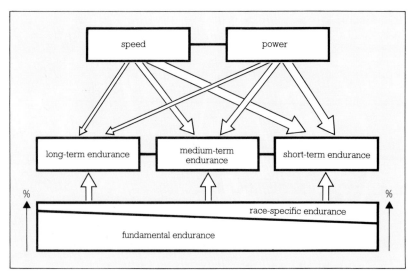

of power in high gears (such as 53/16 or 53/15) and a high number of pedal revolutions (90–110 per minute). It is also possible to undertake this type of training in stages using the 'interval method', in which each period of effort should last 45–120 seconds (short duration) or 2–10 minutes (medium duration). The shorter the period of effort, the higher the speed can be. Lactic acid develops during this kind of anaerobic training and must be broken down by cycling at a slow speed in low gears during the 'rest' periods between the fast, powerful phases.

Power-endurance fibres are a little thicker than the thin, pure ST fibres but they also have a higher aerobic capacity than FT fibres and have a high number of mitochondria so that their maximum endurance capacity can, to a certain degree, be maintained or even improved in spite of the thickening of the muscles.

Speed endurance means resistance to fatigue from heavy speed loads, and is achieved through training with high to maximum speeds. This means cycling in high gears and with a high number of pedal revolutions, as would be needed during sprints, breaking away from a group or in track races. The anaerobic system of energy formation with the development of lactic acid predominates. Stretches of 400–1000m with persistently high speed and a high number of pedal revolutions (110–120 per minute) are covered during speed-endurance training. The speed is similar to race speed.

Endurance-training Methods

Basic or fundamental endurance is, as its name suggests, the most important form of endurance. This kind of endurance is built up with low to medium intensity of whatever type of training is being undertaken; this level of endurance is ample for those who cycle for recreational or health reasons.

Endurance-training methods

Training method	Training content	Level of intensity
endurance performance method	even speed over long distances	I–III
	slight change of speed or cycle-play according to terrain	II–III
interval method	long-term intervals (over 10 minutes)	IV
	medium-term intervals (2–10 minutes)	V
	short-term intervals (45–120 seconds)	VI
repeat method	cycling at race speed or faster	VI
race method	racing	IV–V

More competitive cyclists will build a more or less racing-specific endurance on top of this fundamental endurance. Training for both power and speed endurance will form a part of this additional endurance. The majority of the training should, however, aim to develop fundamental endurance and so achieve a large breathing capacity as well as an optimal development of fat metabolism. There are basically three different types of endurance-training methods:

1. The endurance-performance method: long, continuous sessions of cycle play and hill training (*see* below).
2. Interval methods: long-term intervals, medium-term intervals or short-term intervals.
3. Recovery method: race method.

Continual training using the endurance performance method

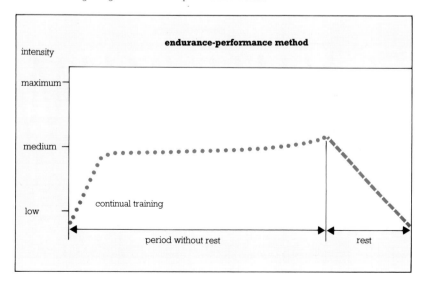

Training

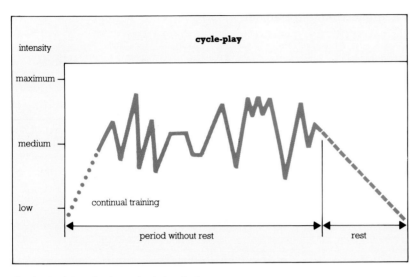

Continual training using the 'cycle-play' method

Endurance-performance Method

The efficacy of continuous endurance loads with low to medium intensity has again been confirmed by modern tests. This method develops, in particular, fundamental endurance, the actual cycling movement and the psychological familiarisation gained from covering a route at an even speed. The minimum duration should be 30 minutes but 1–2 hours is preferable. (Advanced cyclists train in this way for a number of hours.) Small to medium gears (42/18 to 42/16) with a high number of pedal revolutions are used for this kind of training. This develops the maximum oxygen uptake and, from a biochemical point of view, the fat metabolism is 'exercised'.

Speed is maintained over a longer period in the *continuing method*. The so-called Swedish cycle play, or fartlek, is a training device which relies upon changing your speed. This occurs naturally in cycling because of the terrain so you can increase your speed before a climb and decrease it before place-name signs changing down to a lower gear in the process. The combined effect of this type of training is roughly equivalent to that of endurance training.

A more specialised type of training is hill training, during which a number of long hills must be included in a training schedule (load). This form of training requires a larger input of power and strengthens not only leg muscles but also back and trunk muscles. Mountain-pass rides, in particular, require this kind of training preparation. A cyclist should always ensure, however, that this kind of training is followed by re-laxed training on level ground so that the legs do not become too 'heavy' and the round pedal action does not go astray.

Interval Methods

In interval methods, training loads and recovery phases alternate according to a plan in which the recovery phases become so short that the body has in-sufficient time to recover. In other words the new load starts before the recovery is complete, meaning that the pulse does not usually sink lower than 130 beats a minute. A single load lasts 45–120 seconds in the *short-term interval method*, 2–10 minutes in the *medium-term interval method* and over 10 minutes in the *long-term interval method*. The shorter the duration of the load, the larger the intensity should be. Speed endurance may be particularly developed by the short-term interval method and fundamental endurance and racing-specific endurance by the long-term interval method.

When interval loads are ridden with high intensity (at high speed) they are called *intensive interval loads* and when ridden with less intensity (at a lower speed) they are called *extensive interval loads*. Some scientists claim that interval loads result in an increased amount of blood in the heart during the

The interval method; a series of loads with rests (only incomplete recuperation within the loads).

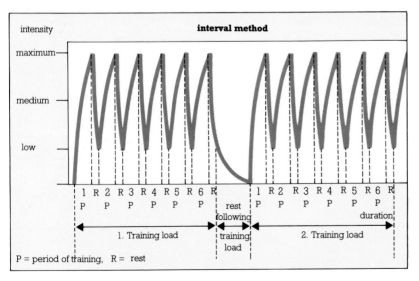

recovery phases. This increased amount may result in the stretching of the heart and promote the development of an enlarged sportsperson's heart.

Well-trained cyclists use interval-training after breaks from training in order to regain their form quickly. It is important to bear in mind, however, that every interval-training load requires 'strong nerves' – so that the time for recuperation after interval-training should last for 72 hours as the nervous system takes longer to recover than the other systems of the body. This is particularly the case with younger cyclists.

Recovery Method

In this method the loads required in a race are repeated at precise intervals so that the body can recover entirely during the rest periods. The speed should either correspond to or slightly exceed race speed. The duration of these 'speed-rides' varies but a useful guide is about 2–5 minutes. The ratio used and the number of pedal revolutions should also match those of a race. Racing-specific endurance, power endurance and speed endurance are all developed in addition to simple speed itself.

Race Method

It is necessary to review and adapt the requirements of training loads and to check performance improvement at regular intervals during the training schedule. The actual methods for racing and checking will depend upon the type of race. Indeed, competitive cyclists polish up on their training by taking part in races and, generally speaking, cyclists should initially participate in some 'build-up' races so that they can work towards their major race of the year. An analysis of the race results will uncover weaknesses and indicates how the training programme can be improved.

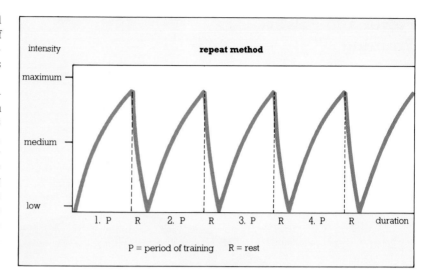

Repeat method (speed training); long rests lead to complete recuperation.

Powerful pedalling during the race – the finish is near.

Training

Power and Power Training

Cyclists must differentiate between two types of power training which are basically:

1. Training of the working muscles specifically used in cycling.

2. Equalising power training of the other muscles.

These two different kinds of training should be kept distinct and undertaken in completely different ways.

Training of the Working Muscles specific to Cycle Sport

There are differences between maximum power, speed power and power endurance, as indicated here:

Maximum power is the power which

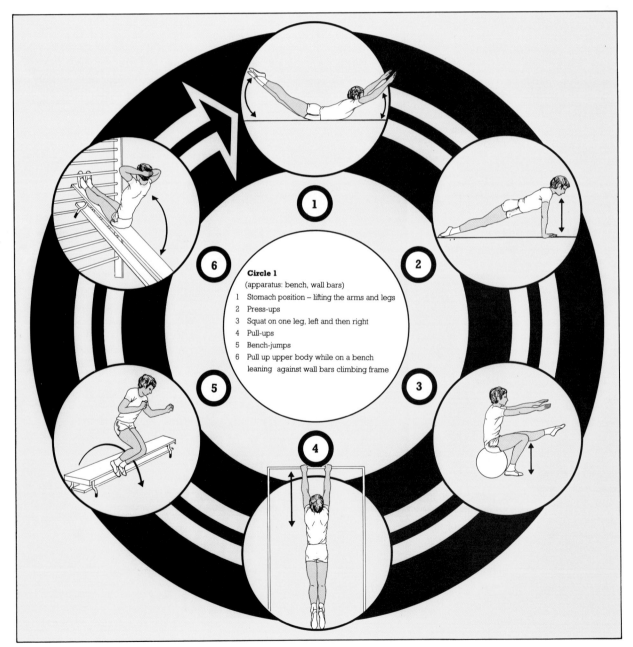

Circle 1

(apparatus: bench, wall bars)

1. Stomach position – lifting the arms and legs
2. Press-ups
3. Squat on one leg, left and then right
4. Pull-ups
5. Bench-jumps
6. Pull up upper body while on a bench leaning against wall bars climbing frame

can be fully developed to the maximum, *speed power* is the ability to overcome high resistances at a high speed and *power endurance* is a resistance against fatigue during long-term power performance.

Power endurance is a special form of endurance and has already been discussed on previous pages. A high degree of both maximum and speed power is required from the cyclist at the start of a race or of training. A force of 350–380kg is transmitted over the pedals, for example, during track races – and at high speeds. (Speed power is, incidentally, necessary for any sports discipline.) In cycling an increase in maximum and speed power should, if possible, occur without any increase in the thickness of the muscle fibres. Moreover, speed power should be de-veloped in a cycling-specific manner so that it can be turned into energy – training the leg muscles in a gymnasium has, interestingly, proved to be ineffective. It is much more beneficial to develop them either when cycling or perhaps on a 'home trainer'. Small to medium resistances are used for this with a high number of pedal revolutions.

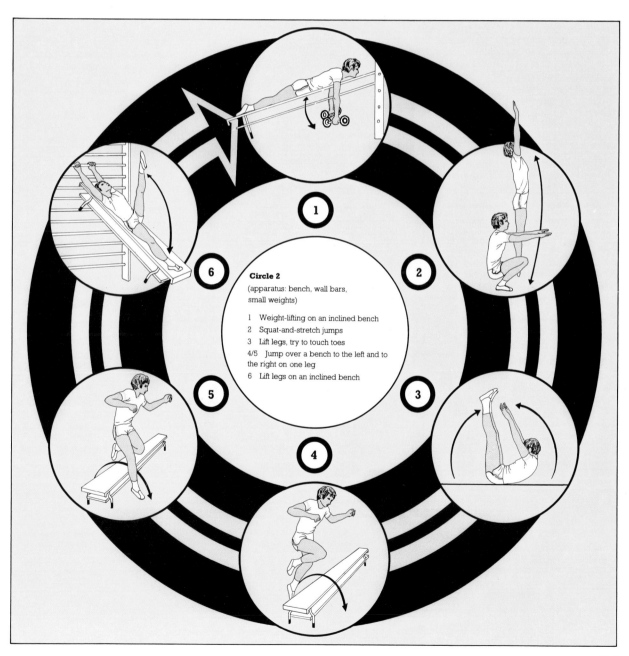

Circle 2

(apparatus: bench, wall bars, small weights)

1 Weight-lifting on an inclined bench
2 Squat-and-stretch jumps
3 Lift legs, try to touch toes
4/5 Jump over a bench to the left and to the right on one leg
6 Lift legs on an inclined bench

Training

Methods of Cycling-Specific Power Training

Maximum power is increased when high gears are pushed with 80–100 per cent of the entire amount of power. These loads are practised by undertaking sprints of 20–30 seconds each, between two and eight sprints forming a series. You should recover fully after each of these sprints. This type of heavy power load requires complete concentration and so they should only be undertaken at the beginning of a training session.

During speed-power training both the number of pedal revolutions and the maximum power should be improved. However, the difficulty with this is that the more you use maximum power, the lower will be the number of pedal revolutions achieved – and vice versa; the more you exercise speed, the less you develop maximum power. In speed-power training you must concentrate on reaching a very high number of pedal revolutions.

The loads for maximum and speed-power training should not be so heavy that the actual cycling style suffers as a result. You should reduce the load if the round pedal-action loses its smoothness as this will result in either a reduction in the input of power or in the number of pedal revolutions.

Equalising Power Training for the Cyclist

The muscles, with the exception of the leg muscles which are strengthened on the ergometer or the exercise bicycle, should be strengthened through particular exercises, especially the muscles of the back, stomach and trunk. It is not important to develop a large mass of muscles – but rather to improve the quality and capacity of the existing muscles. Training with little resistance (or small weights) serves this purpose

Lie on your back on a bench, feet on the ground and stretch your arms to the sides. Lift your outstretched arms up until your hands are as far apart as your shoulders.

Using a large weight in an inclined position, pull the weight towards the chest as far as possible so that your elbows are on a level with your shoulders. The body should not be moved backwards.

Use the pulling apparatus with one hand, then the other, keeping the body still.

and allows ten or twenty repetitions of each exercise. Power training should always be a secondary aim – and never become an end in itself. One or two power-training sessions per week are sufficient during the winter and during the summer, one – preferably supplemented by some morning exercises – will suffice. Pages 112 and 113 show two possibilities of circuit training which are quite easy to build up.

Exercises

These numbers refer to the illustrations on pages 116 and 117.

1. Move the head alternately to the left and to the right.
2. Circle the shoulders.
3. Circle the arms.
4. Bend the trunk so that the hands touch the ground. Keep the legs straight and then raise the trunk lifting the arms.
5. Bend sideways with the hands under the head and without twisting the trunk. Repeat to the other side.
6. With the legs apart, bend and twist the trunk forwards; one hand touches the opposite foot, swinging the other hand upwards.
7. Spread the legs as far as possible and bend the trunk forwards then hold the ankles with the hands and push the trunk downwards.
8. With the legs still far apart, bend the trunk forwards and, with the arms folded, try to touch the ground with the elbows, then raise the trunk.
9. Stretch one leg sideways, bend the other and lower the hips as far as possible before changing sides.
10. Circle the foot a number of times both clockwise and anti-clockwise before repeating with the other foot.
11. Bend and twist the trunk backwards with the legs apart; try to reach one heel with the opposite hand while the other hand is raised forwards to help maintain balance.
12. Forward press-ups; bend and stretch arms keeping hips straight (about 10–20 times).

Lying on your back, hold on to the wall bars (or the base of a cupboard), lift your legs first and then all of the body, reaching as high as possible with your feet.

Lying on your back on an inclined bench, wedge your feet underneath a bar and bend your knees slightly, placing your hands behind your head. Lift the body, moving your chest towards your knees.

Lying on your back, hold a ball in your hands. Lift the body up and bend forwards, placing the ball between your feet.

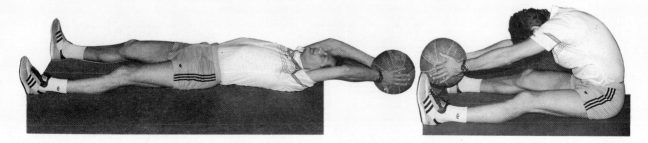

Training

Speed and Speed Training

Speed within cycling can be broken down into reaction speed, pedal power and pedalling speed, all resulting in forward movement. This speed is produced from the combined actions of the central nervous system and muscle power. The fundamental speed depends upon the type of the muscles (FT or ST fibres), the quality of the actual movement (the round pedal-action), the relaxation ability and whether or not the muscles are 'warmed up' as well as general alertness. Maximum speed cannot, of course, be reached when a cyclist is tired. This is why speed training should be undertaken only at the beginning of a training session and preferably using the recovery method so that there can be a complete recuperation after each training load.

Speed is practised by sprinting with maximum pedal revolutions (120–160 per minute) in small-to-medium gears (for instance 42/16 or 42/15). Each sprint should cover around 100–250m, 3–5 of these forming a series. The recovery period after each sprint is around 3–4 minutes. A total of 2–4 of these series forms one training session. The input of power should only be sufficiently great to apply a little pressure on the pedals. Speed training also improves the quality of the nervous system in the muscles as well as improving the energy supply through the abundance of energy-rich phosphates.

Suppleness and Suppleness Training

Suppleness – or flexibility – is more important to the cyclist than is generally appreciated. The goal of suppleness training is to create a wide range of movement in the individual joints. It is easier to increase performance when the movement of a particular joint is relaxed and free and this is only possible if the joint is not stretched to the limit of its capacity. All cyclists should maintain – or even improve – the flexibility of their spine, particularly in the region of the lumbar vertebrae and the neck as the action of cycling affects these areas – especially on the racing bicycle. Flexibility training can be carried out in different ways, for instance by:

1. Early morning exercises.
2. Stretching.
3. Yoga.

Stretching exercises should push you to the limit of your range of mobility particularly in the region of the spine, hips, knees and ankles. Every cyclist should devise a training routine for the improvement of their flexibility. There is a fundamental principle which says 'Human beings are as young as their joints'.

Training Programme

Training should always be planned. Monotonous training without consideration of the fundamental principles in the long run has no beneficial effects upon a cyclist's performance. Training loads should be increased with an increase in performance in order to make training both effective and exciting. Enthusiasm for training should continue throughout the year with your

Flexibility is important for every sports discipline. It also builds up 'movement reserves' for the joints and improves their function.

The training year for cycling

Nov	Dec	Jan	Feb	Mar	Apr	May	Jun	Jul	Aug	Sep	Oct
introductory mesocycle	fundamental mesocycle 1		fundamental mesocycle 2		mesocycle prior to racing	racing mesocycle 1	racing mesocycle 2	restorative and preparatory mesocycle	racing mesocycle 3	restorative mesocycle	
preparation period						race period					transition period

performance not remaining constant all the year around. This is why the load requirements should be built up cyclically and periodically according to a certain rhythm. The degree of awareness is important, too, inasmuch as you should know why you are training in a certain manner and not in any other; this also will increase the effect of training.

The Principle of Progressive Training

You must appreciate from the outset that training is a biological development which requires a certain amount of time. Only a training programme which builds up systematically, patiently and over a long period of time according to the principle of progressive training will last and be stable. A novice must have the patience to develop his or her performance over a period of 3–5 years (if training is undertaken regularly, throughout the year and over a number of years). The performance of novices who are too impatient, who train at too high an intensity too soon and for too long will stagnate – or even deteriorate.

It is also important to remember that breaks from training of a week or more result in the loss of 'adaptation'; in other words, you will have to start from near the beginning once again. You should supplement your programme with ad-

ditional training during the winter and in bad weather as your personal best can only be improved by continual and regular training throughout the year.

The training process for young people will take even longer, if they want to reach the top. In the development of a racing cyclist there are distinct stages which may be described as follows:

1. Preparation stage (12–15 years).
2. Build-up stage (16–18 years).
3. Specialist stage (19 onwards).
4. Time of first international success (19–21 years).
5. Optimal performance stage (22–26 years).
6. Consistent maximum performance stage (27–30 years).

You can expect a training process of around 10–12 years, in other words, for the full development of a racing cyclist. How long racing cyclists are able to maintain their maximum performance after the age of 30 depends largely upon their lifestyle and upon training methods with planned phases for recuperation and healthy eating. Racing cyclists may thus be successful in highly competitive sport until over the age of 40.

On a lower level (moderately competitive cycling) there is enough proof that it is perfectly possible to embark upon cycling after the age of 30 and still be successful in veterans' races after 4–5 years' training – even until the age of 50 or 60.

Yoga Exercises

Hatha-yoga is an ideal type of movement training for the spinal cord. Concentration and breathing techniques also improve the effect of the exercises. An example of a yoga session is given on pages 120 and 121:

1. **The triangle.** One hand slides sideways down the leg while the other arm is stretched upwards.
2. **The candle.** Support the back with the hands and stretch body completely up as high as possible.
3. **The plough.** The feet touch the ground behind the head, if possible, keeping the legs straight.
4. **The knee–forehead pose.** The sole of one foot touches the other leg with the heel lying close to the groin. The hands touch the other foot and the forehead touches the knee.
5. **The pliers.** Sit with the legs stretched out and bend the trunk so that the forehead touches the knees.
6. **The fish.** Fold the legs and bend the trunk backwards until the head touches the ground.
7. **The snake.** Lie flat on the stomach and raise the trunk, supporting the position with slightly bent arms.
8. **The grasshopper.** Lie on the stomach, lifting the feet and holding them still while keeping the hands under the hips with palms facing the ground.
9. **The half-circle.** Lie on the stomach, grip the ankles and stretch the spinal cord.
10. **The twist.** Position one foot across the opposite, bent leg, the hand behind the back gripping the other hand which passes under the knee.
11. **The headstand.** The head and forearms form an isosceles triangle. The body rests on the forehead and forearms.
12. **The dead man.** Relax lying on the back, keeping the eyes closed.

Training

An example of training using an ergometer (home trainer)

minutes	type of training	pedal revolutions (per minute)	pedalling resistance	level of intensity
1–5	warm-up	100–110	low	low (I–II)
6	level I	100	medium	medium to
7		105		intensive (III–IV)
8		110		
9		115		
10		120		
11–15	level II	as level I	as level I	as level I
16–20	level III	as level I	as level I	as level I
21–25	level IV	as level I	as level I	as level I
26–30	conclusion	100–110	low	low

A good ergometer should have a large wheel, stability, an adjustable sitting position, equipment to measure both the number of pedal revolutions per minute, and the pulse.

Suggested accessories: ventilator; tape recorder; watch; mirror (for the observation of riding style).

The Cyclic Nature of the Training Programme

The adaptation to an increased capacity occurs in the following phases of the training process:

1. The adaptation to the sports capacity (an increase in performance).

2. The stabilising of the sports capacity (a levelling of performance).
3. A temporary decrease in performance.

This is why you should not train at the same level throughout the year but determine the intensity, according to quantity and nature of the load over certain periods of time (cycles).

1. 'Macrocycles' – usually annual but also six-monthly and several-year cycles.
2. 'Mesocycles' – also called stages – a term of 3–6 weeks.
3. 'Microcycles' – cycles lasting one week or less broken down into single training units.

Long-term Cycle (macrocycle)

One macrocycle usually covers the training for one year. The training loads are broken up into micro- and mesocycles and lined up methodically within the macrocycle so that you reach one or more performance peaks. Within cycling the training year is divided up into the following stages:

1. Preparation period:
   (a) winter training;
   (b) spring training.
2. Race period:
   (a) first mesocycle;
   (b) stabilising phase one;
   (c) second mesocycle;
   (d) stabilising phase two;
   (e) third mesocycle.
3. Transition period.

An example of a training plan for one week's winter training

Type of training	The aim of training	Notes	Frequency per week
cycling (road training)	aerobic fundamental endurance	about 1–2 hours, according to weather conditions warm clothing	1–2 times
ergometer (home trainer)	round pedal-action technique training	about 30–40 minutes high pedalling frequency	2–3 times
cross-country run	aerobic fundamental endurance	about 30–60 minutes	2–3 times
circuit-training games	general fitness	about one hour	once
power training	development of stomach, back, shoulders and chest muscles	small weights or resistances no work above the head 10–20 repeats of every exercise	once

Training indoors on rollers with adjustable resistance.

A home trainer (ergometer) with a large wheel suitable for cycle-sport training.

A week's training plan for competitive cyclists (for instance during the spring)

Monday	morning; relaxed endurance training (small gears) afternoon; 2–3 hours of regenerative training
Tuesday	morning; anaerobic training, 90–120 minutes afternoon; relaxed endurance training 2–3 hours (aerobic)
Wednesday	long endurance training (180–220km) aerobic (with food)
Thursday	intensive endurance training with change in rhythm (aerobic–anaerobic border)
Friday	morning: relaxed regenerative training, 2 hours afternoon: relaxed endurance training, 2–3 hours (small gears)
Saturday	slow, relaxed cycling, 1–2 hours race preparation, checking of equipment

Preparation Period (November to April)

The basic fitness for the summer period is founded during the preparation period – which lasts six months. The type of training undertaken depends upon weather conditions and so it is important to have a number of different training facilities at your disposal, so keeping the training programme flexible.

Winter Training (November to February)

The aim of this training is to improve overall fitness, to minimise the weaknesses of the body, to build up fundamental endurance and to practise the perfect, round pedal-action. Training which is specific to cycling (such as road training, 'home-training', cross-country cycling and mountain biking) serves as suitable training as do general athletic training (such as cross-country running, skiing, circuit training, ball games and swimming) and power and flexibility training (exercises, stretching and yoga).

Spring Training (February to April)

Spring starts on 21 March according to the British calendar but usually much later according to the British weather. This period is nevertheless called spring training and many European cyclists travel to countries such as Italy, the south of France, southern Spain or Mallorca during this time (usually in February or March) in order to improve their fundamental endurance in spring conditions. The beneficial effects of air rich with iodine from the proximity of the sea and the psychologically exciting feeling of foreign surroundings should not be underestimated – especially when you compare the blossom with the wind, rain and snow of home. The training quantity should be steadily increased at a low or medium intensity (25–30kmh) involving long training rides with a low ratio (42/18 to 42/16) which develops both the fundamental endurance and metabolism of fat. If you train abroad, you must continue the programme on your return not forgetting that you will need plenty of clothing to protect yourself from the cold which will be noticeable in comparison with the warmth of southern Europe.

The increased use of the maximum oxygen intake during training (after Astrand and Rodahl).

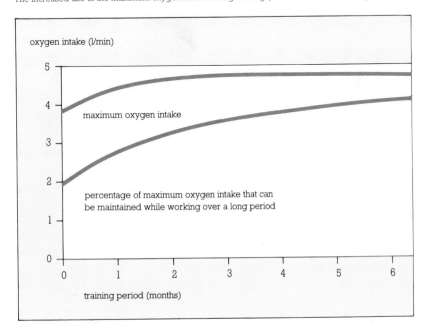

Training

Racing cyclists increase their training intensity towards the end of their spring training and cycle in higher gears from time to time in order to improve their power endurance and so gradually become accustomed to racing speed.

Racing Period (summer training)

Recreational cyclists should follow their fundamental endurance training by cycling at a low to medium intensity, occasionally increasing the quantity by cycling longer distances (perhaps at the weekend). You should, however, deliberately undertake 'regenerating' training units of low intensity after hard touring or heavy training sessions.

More serious cyclists and competitive cyclists in particular must work towards a higher speed (that is a further increase in and greater use of the current maximum breathing capacity). For this reason the race period is divided up into two or three mesocycles, each lasting about four to six weeks. You begin with comparatively easy build-up races in the first mesocycle (May/June). Indeed the amount of training can be slightly decreased because there will be an increase in intensity during races. A phase of *stabilising* then follows. Cyclists participate in a greater number of more competitive races during the second and third mesocycles (July/September) in order to ensure that their best condition is reached at the right time. The quantity of training can be further decreased during this time. Race-specific training is increasingly important. Racing cyclists who participate in national and international races prepare themselves by riding hard stage-races, in order to ensure that their best capacity can be developed.

Transition Period (regeneration period)

A minimum of four to six weeks' recuperation or regeneration should follow the months of maximum load during the race period in order to allow the body to become receptive to winter training.

Medium-term Cycle (mesocycle)

In training periods lasting three to six weeks you need to adapt the load to the current capacity because in this period the performance may develop erratically. A recognised principle of training is always to increase the quantity of training first – and then the intensity. Phases of heavier loads should be alternated with phases of light loads. It is also occasionally necessary within competitive cycling to increase the intensity of a load within a mesocycle so much that the limits of the current capacity are reached in order to trigger off further adaptation processes. This will be necessary, for example, in the mesocycle immediately preceding a major event.

Short-term Cycle (microcycle)

A microcycle covers the training of one week and is split up into single training units. This short-term planning is of great importance as the long-term training schedule is only successful if the short-term planning is properly followed.

The sum of the single training units determines the quality of the entire training programme. You should never be complacent in your training but concentrate on every single training unit as alertness increases the effectiveness of the training load.

Every training unit should consist of the following three components:

1. Warm-up.
2. Core.
3. Cool-down.

The body is physically and emotionally prepared for the core of the training during the first part, the warm-up, which should last fifteen to twenty minutes. In this you should cycle in low gears and in a relaxed fashion in order

Weekly training programme for competitive cyclists during the race period

Monday	regenerative training (active recuperation): medium quantity, low intensity, technique practice
Tuesday	intensive endurance training with long-term intervals: training to develop fundamental endurance, power endurance and speed
Wednesday	fundamental-endurance training: high quantity of training, low intensity, technique practice
Thursday	intensive endurance training with speed training: high quantity, high intensity, long-term and middle-term intervals, medium-gears with high pedalling speed
Friday	regenerative training (active recuperation): high quantity, low intensity, technique practice
Saturday	fundamental-endurance training with power- endurance training: medium quantity, high intensity, medium to high gears, high pedalling frequency
Sunday	intensive endurance training: high quantity, high intensity

to prepare for the actual training. This will stimulate both the circulation and the metabolism. The small blood vessels (capillaries) dilate, the muscles become more flexible, movement becomes more flowing and the body temperature rises. The likelihood of enjoying the training unit is also increased.

The training load is carried out in the 'core' of the unit according to the training plan. Training loads which require mental alertness and concentration such as speed training, sprints, interval-training and so forth should, in principle, be carried out in the first half of the training unit and endurance training can follow in the second half.

Regeneration is encouraged during the cool-down part of the training session through active recuperation and so this aspect of training is just as important as the warm-up in preparation for the training. You should cycle in a relaxed state and in medium to small gears to loosen the entire body – you should also be happy to have completed the training session in an optimal fashion. Indeed it is very important to conclude every session in a happy and cheerful frame of mind.

Training Diary

Almost every athlete in competitive sport keeps a training diary which can be more or less detailed, depending upon the choice of the individual. Regular notes promote both training discipline and the conscientiousness required to follow the programme correctly. They also help training control and record any useful personal experiences – you can learn a great deal from past experiences and mistakes and so can adapt future training measures. Cyclists who have enjoyed success by

The build-up for the race period

cycle	structure	main aims
first cycle (about 4–8 weeks)	gradual introduction to optimal race frequency; build up races with an increase in the level of difficulty; one or two major races towards the end of the cycle; the amount of load during training varies according to race frequency; the load is slightly reduced	quick improvement in race performance; development of race 'toughness'; recognition of weaknesses and reserves; gathering of race experience and testing of tactical principles; strengthening of techniques under race conditions
first stabilising phase (1–2 weeks)	regenerative training	'toughening' of the training conditions
second cycle (about 4 weeks)	training is even more important; an increase in the quantity and the load of training; small number of races; no decrease in training.	overcoming of the weaknesses recognised during the past races
second stabilising phase (1–2 weeks)	regenerative training	'toughening' of the training conditions
third cycle (about 4 weeks)	races with a higher degree of difficulty than those during the first cycle (build-up races for qualifying for competition); gradual reduction of the quantity of the load during training	Stabilising at race fitness; preparation for qualifying races; proving yourself in particularly tough race conditions

It is quite possible to train out of doors during the winter provided you wear proper cycle clothing – as shown in this illustration of a cross-country race held in the winter.

Training

following a training programme probably want to be able to look back on it.
Simple training notes should at least
contain the number of kilometres covered and the training load. Further useful notes might include the morning
resting pulse, a description of your
general well-being, average cycle
speed and the gear ratio most used.
Only written notes can record adequately whether or not the training programme was followed – and whether
or not you train according to your
plans. Again, only written notes will re-
veal weaknesses over a long period of
time – the first step in overcoming
them in the future. A training diary promotes the discipline necessary for an
athlete's way of life.

Good Condition

The aim of a training programme is, in
principle, to reach your maximum potential and to maintain it, once it has
been reached, by carrying out the right
training loads. Training which develops
and maintains a good condition will ultimately have different aims for recreational, competitive, girl, women, junior
and veteran cyclists. Accordingly, the
following training programmes designed to develop good condition have
been divided up into three different
groups, each aimed at a different level.

1.   Training programme I – for junior
cyclists (16–18 years), girls, women,
veterans and touring cyclists all of
whom aim to participate in short races
of 60, 80 or 100km.
2.   Training programme II – for amateurs who wish to participate in races of
150–220km.

Training Programme I

(devised by G. Ambrosini)

Week	Day	Distance	Gear ratio	Type of training
1	Monday	15km on the flat	42/20 or 48/22	speed 20 kmh
	Tuesday	20km on the flat		control of the sitting position
	Thursday	20km on the flat	fixed wheel	practice of cycling style
	Sunday	30km on the flat		easy, relaxed cycling
2	Monday	20km on the flat	as above	speed 21–23kmh
	Tuesday	25km on the flat	as above	practice of cycling style
	Thursday	25km on the flat	as above	
	Sunday	40km on the flat	as above	easy, relaxed cycling
3	Monday	25km on the flat	42/19 or 48/21	speed 24–26kmh
	Tuesday	30km on the flat		practice of cycling style
	Thursday	30km on the flat	fixed wheel	short sprints, finishing spurts
	Sunday	50km on the flat		easy, relaxed cycling
4	Monday	30km with short, gentle gradients	as above	speed 26–28kmh
	Tuesday	as above	as above	practice of cycling style increased number of sprints, finishing spurts
	Thursday	35km with short, gentle gradients	as above	
	Sunday	60km "	very low gears	easy, relaxed cycling
5	Monday	35km, gradients up to 5%	42/17 or 48/19	speed 27–29kmh, fast starts, increased number of sprints
	Tuesday	40km "	42/18 or 48/20	intermediate spurts, finishing spurts
	Thursday	40km "	42/19 or 48/21	
	Sunday	80km "	as above	easy, relaxed cycling
6	Monday	40km, gradients up to 7%	42/16 or 48/18	speed 30kmh, training content as for week 5
	Tuesday	45km "	42/17 or 48/19	
	Thursday	45km "	42/19 or 48/21	
	Sunday	90km "	42/20 or 48/22	easy, relaxed cycling
7	Monday	45km, with varying gradients	42/15 or 48/17	speed 31–32kmh, training content as above
	Tuesday	50km "	42/16 or 48/18	
	Thursday	50km "	42/18 or 48/20	
	Sunday	100km "	42/19 or 48/21	easy, relaxed cycling
8	Monday	50km, with varying gradients	42/15 or 48/16	speed 33–34kmh, training content as above
	Tuesday	50km "	42/15 or 48/17	
	Thursday	50km "	42/17 or 48/19	
	Sunday	100km "	42/19 or48/21	easy, relaxed cycling
9	Monday	50km, with gentle gradients	as for week 8	speed high to maximum
	Tuesday	30km on the flat		as above
	Thursday	20km on the flat		as above
	Sunday	race		as above

The gears quoted are based upon the average gear system. You can cycle with the usual
small chainwheel (42 teeth) or choose a 'smaller' large chainwheel at the beginning of training
during the build-up period. This chainwheel will have 48 rather than 53 teeth.

3. Training programme III – for advanced amateurs or professional cyclists who wish to participate in arduous races of 160–180km.

Indicators of Good Condition

All cyclists should be able to tell, by self-observation, when they have reached their personal best. There are certain signs of good condition – signs which show that you have trained correctly:

1. Easy and correct pedalling; a willingness and ability to gain speed quickly.
2. A feeling of general good health and energy, a good appetite, eupepsia, restful sleep, feeling of freshness on waking, being calm and in a good frame of mind, self confidence.
3. A loss of weight not exceeding 1kg even after intensive training.
4. The body-weight at which you achieve most success is your ideal race weight; you should note this and aim for it every year.
5. A thin layer of subcutaneous fatty tissue, particularly so over the triceps and shoulders (when measured by skin-fold callipers it should be 6mm or less).
6. A slow resting pulse (in recreational cycling this will be around 60 beats per minute, in competitive sport at or less than 50 beats a minute and in highly competitive sport around or under 40 beats a minute); quick relaxation of the pulse after training loads.
7. Low blood pressure (usually between 120/70mmHg and 100/60mmHg for competitive cyclists).
8. Calm breathing.
9. The capacity to sweat profusely when undertaking vigorous exercise and good heat tolerance.
10. A feeling of ease during training as if the bicycle were rolling of its own accord – and you only need to guide it.

Training Programme II

(devised by G. Ambrosini)

Week	Day	Distance	Gear ratio	Type of training
1	Monday	25km on the flat	42/20 or 48/22	speed 20kmh
	Tuesday	30km on the flat		control of the sitting position
	Thursday	30km on the flat	fixed wheel	practice of cycling style
	Sunday	40km on the flat		easy, relaxed cycling
2	Monday	30km on the flat	as above	speed 21–23kmh
	Tuesday	35km on the flat	as above	practice of cycling style
	Thursday	35km on the flat	as above	
	Sunday	50km on the flat	as above	easy, relaxed cycling
3	Monday	35km on the flat	42/19 or 48/21	speed 24–26kmh
	Tuesday	40km on the flat		practice of cycling style
	Thursday	40km on the flat	fixed wheel	short sprints, finishing spurts
	Sunday	60km on the flat		easy, relaxed cycling
4	Monday	40 km with gentle gradients	as above	speed 27–28kmh, increased number of sprints, finishing spurts
	Tuesday	50km ''	as above	
	Thursday	50km ''	as above	
	Sunday	80km ''	as above	easy, relaxed cycling
5	Monday	50km, gradients up to 5%	very low gears, 42/17 or 48/19	speed 29–30kmh, sprints, intermediate spurts, finishing sprints
	Tuesday	60km ''	42/18 or 48/20	
	Thursday	60km ''	42/19 or 48/21	
	Sunday	100km ''	as above	easy, relaxed cycling
6	Monday	60km, gradients up to 7%	42/16 or 48/18	speed 31–32kmh, training content as for week 5
	Tuesday	70km ''	42/17 or 48/19	
	Thursday	70km ''	42/19 or 48/21	
	Sunday	120km ''	42/20 or 48/22	easy, relaxed cycling
7	Monday	70km, with varying gradients	42/15 or 48/17	speed 33–34kmh, training content as above
	Tuesday	80km ''	42/16 or 48/18	
	Thursday	80km ''	42/18 or 48/20	
	Sunday	120km ''	42/19 or 48/21	easy, relaxed cycling
8	Monday	80km, with varying gradients	42/16 or 48/18	speed 33–34kmh, training content as above
	Tuesday	100km ''	42/15 or 48/17	
	Thursday	80km ''	42/17 or 48/19	
	Sunday	80km ''	42/19 or 48/21	easy, relaxed cycling
9	Monday	80km, with varying gradients	as above	speed high to maximum training content as above
	Tuesday	50km ''	as above	
	Thursday	30km ''	as above	
	Sunday	race		

Training

Training Programme III

(devised by G. Ambrosini)

Week	Day	Distance	Gear ratio	Type of training
1	Monday	30km on the flat	42/19 or 29/22	speed 23kmh
	Tuesday	35km on the flat		control of the sitting position
	Thursday	35km on the flat	fixed wheel	practice of cycling style
	Sunday	50km on the flat		easy, relaxed style
2	Monday	35km on the flat	as above	speed 25–26kmh
	Tuesday	40km on the flat	as above	practice of technique and style
	Thursday	40km on the flat	as above	
	Sunday	70km on the flat	as above	easy, relaxed style
3	Monday	45km on the flat	42/18 or 49/21	speed 27–28kmh
	Tuesday	60km on the flat	42/18 or 49/21	practice of technique and style
	Thursday	60km on the flat	42/18 or 49/21	short sprints
	Sunday	100km on the flat	42/18 or 49/21	easy, relaxed cycling
4	Monday	60km with gentle gradients	42/17 or 49/20	speed 27–28kmh, increased number of sprints, finishing spurts
	Tuesday	80km ''	42/17 or 49/20	
	Thursday	80km ''	42/17 or 49/20	
	Sunday	120km ''	42/17 or 49/20	easy, relaxed cycling
5	Monday	80km, gradients up to 5%	very low gears, 42/16 or 49/19	speed 30kmh, quick starts, increased number of sprints,
	Tuesday	90km ''	42/17 or 49/20	intermediate spurts, finishing sprints
	Thursday	90km ''	42/80 or 49/21	
	Sunday	140km ''	42/19 or 49/22	easy, relaxed cycling
6	Monday	90km, gradients up to 7%	42/15 or 49/18	speed 31–32kmh, quick starts, increased number of sprints
	Tuesday	100km ''	42/16 or 49/19	intermediate spurts, finishing sprints
	Thursday	100km ''	42/18 or 49/21	
	Sunday	150km ''	42/19 or 49/22	easy, relaxed cycling
7	Monday	100km, gradients up to 10%	53/18 or 49/17	speed 33–34kmh, quick starts, increased number of sprints
	Tuesday	120km ''	42/16 or 49/19	intermediate spurts, finishing sprints
	Thursday	120km ''	42/18 or 49/21	
	Sunday	150km ''	42/19 or 49/22	easy, relaxed cycling
8	Monday	120km, with varying gradients	53/17 or 49/16	speed 33–36kmh, quick starts, increased number of sprints, intermediate spurts
	Tuesday	150km ''	53/18 or 49/17	
	Thursday	120km ''	42/16 or 49/19	
	Sunday	150km ''	42/18 or 49/21	easy, relaxed cycling
9	Monday	120km, with varying gradients	as above	speed high to maximum, training content as above
	Tuesday	80km ''	as above	
	Thursday	40km ''	as above	
	Sunday	race		

Races give cyclists their final polish, and are also an indication of their level of fitness/abililty.

Maintaining Fitness

Cyclists who are in good condition should maintain their fitness. Training for the maintenance of fitness can be of a lower intensity and quantity than for building it up. Every race demands complete exertion so training to encourage regeneration or recuperation is necessary after races.

You should rest on the day after the race, perhaps taking a warm bath and even a massage. Easy, relaxed training with small gears on the second day can further promote recuperation. You can train at medium intensity for the three following days, taking into account how much effort the load feels. On the day before the next race you should rest, look after yourself and your bicycle and prepare whatever is necessary for the next day.

Cycling for Women and Girls

The participation of women and girls in cycling is continually increasing – and rightly so – they should be encouraged to participate in this wonderful sports discipline. As husbands and boys enjoy taking part in cycling, so should women – allowing the whole family to cycle together. Misconceptions should be pushed aside and fundamental principles laid down regarding the training ability of women.

History

The first road race which included women was held in 1869 on bicycles made from iron and weighing 50kg. Taking twenty-ninth position in the first international road race from Paris to Rouen (a distance of over 123km) was the then Miss America. The first World Cup for women took place in Belgium in 1897.

The American Annie Londonderry completed a special long-distance cycle tour in 1895 when she cycled around the world covering 28,000 miles (45,000km). Six-day races for women have existed since 1895 in the United Kingdom and in the United States. A ladies' team in mixed races once beat their male colleagues. Official international women's road races have existed since 1958 and the number of female cyclists has steadily increased since the inclusion of women's road races in the Olympic games in 1984. The inclusion of a women's marathon has also only come about in re-cent years – indeed it was proven at an earlier stage in cycling than in running that women are quite capable of enduring long and intensive training loads.

Biological Factors

Women are usually lighter than men because they are smaller and because they are generally not so heavily built. Two important differences between the composition of a man's and a woman's body is that the proportion of fatty tissue is larger and the proportion of muscle tissue is smaller in a woman's body. The maximum oxygen uptake per kilogram of body-weight is around

Women are biologically well suited to cycling.

twenty per cent below that of a man (due to the higher proportion of fatty tissue within the female body). Women are physiologically at a disadvantage compared to men when cycling at a high intensity (high speed) because at this level of performance breathing capacity is of vital importance. They are, however, more suited than men to long rides at a low-to-medium intensity – because of their low body-weight. (Women will sometimes be on an equal level to heavier men when both are climbing hills.)

The power capacity of women is less than that of men because, as mentioned earlier, their proportion of muscles is lower. The same also applies to power endurance and so, within cycling, women are at a disadvantage when compared to men whenever there is a need to pedal hard in high gears, for instance when competing in time trials or when riding on flat ground at a fast pace. These disadvantages (when a high input of power is needed) can, however, be partially negated by cycling with a higher number of pedal revolutions per minute. This is why the gears used by female cyclists should be lower than those for males. The top gears during a women's road race are therefore around 52/15 on flat ground.

Women are undoubtedly able to undertake long endurance events with low-to-medium intensity despite those anatomical differences mentioned earlier. The more 'masculine' woman or girl who therefore has a comparatively small amount of fatty tissue and large amount of muscle is probably at an advantage within competitive cycling.

Training Adaptation

Within endurance training the adaptation ability of women is broadly similar to that for men; it is quite possible for the volume of the heart and the oxygen uptake to double through correct training. It is expected that the performance of women within world cycling will further increase in the future as women's cycling is still in its infancy. Recreational cycling gives women – as it does men – the opportunity to build up a good level of fitness, to clear headaches and to lose fatty tissue where it is unwanted because fat dissolves over active muscles like butter melts in the sun.

Training during Childhood and Adolescence

During the last few decades numerous tests have unanimously shown that children's (and adolescents') growth does not occur evenly but rather erratically in alternating periods of fast growth (stretching) and slower growth (filling out). Moreover, in all Western countries there is a trend towards accelerating growth which does not only mean faster growth but also faster physiological maturity and a general increase in height. Capacity and growth are closely linked and so the following conclusions can be drawn from today's knowledge:

1. Practising movement and flexibility should start at the age of 5 years.
2. Fitness abilities – particularly endurance and general athletic development – should be given greater importance for 9–11 year-olds as they provide the necessary stimulus to promote growth.
3. It is quite possible to ask children of 9 years – or perhaps even younger – to carry out endurance performances.
4. Performances involving a maximum input of power should not be carried out by pubertal or pre-pubertal children.

Youths who have undergone comprehensive training are equipped with the same adaptation mechanism as adults. The ability to become fit is even greater in youths before and during puberty than it is for adults using corresponding training loads. Cycling is particularly suitable as a way of developing endurance. Indeed the potential of the young body can be fully developed through cycling; weaknesses of the posture can be corrected and superfluous body-weight can be lost. The information in the following paragraphs should, however, be taken into consideration.

The percentage of general athletic training and specialised cycle training for children and youths as they mature (D. Junker, H. Weisbrod and D. Mickein).

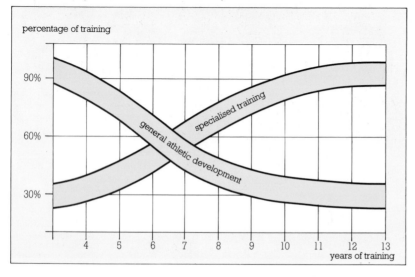

Children and youths should not adopt specialist training too soon but should learn an extensive number of movements and undertake various other types of sport. Specialist cycle training should only be undertaken once or twice a week – and then using small gears and a high number of pedal revolutions (avoiding large gears with a high input of power).

The best opportunity to develop a substantial maximum oxygen uptake occurs during puberty; emphasis should be placed on this if a youth is keen to develop into a racing cyclist. Aerobic capacity in youths is best developed with three types of endurance performance: continuous endurance training; alternate training; and cycle-play. The levels of intensity should be from level 1 to level 3. Parents should be warned about becoming too ambitious for their children – who should never be forced to carry out training loads to which they object. The length of the route ridden can increase with a child's age. On average it can be as long as the following rules:

1. Around 20km at 10 years.
2. Around 30km at 11 years.
3. Around 40–50km at 12 years.
4. Around 50–60km at 13 years.

A longer outing can be undertaken as endurance training once a week – perhaps at the weekend – but only at low-to-medium intensity. (It is for this reason that most national cycling bodies limit the ratio of gears for children and youths. Children and youths should always train in low gears under 60 inches with a high number of pedal revolutions and a low input of power. This is the way to develop fully the cardiorespiratory system, the metabolism and the composition of the muscle fibres).

Children also want to measure their ability in races, but this should be done in a playful and not too competitive manner.

Training _____

Cycling at an Older Age

The ageing of the human body is marked in the following ways:

1. A slowing down and decrease in the ability to adapt to loads.
2. A general decrease in performance.
3. A decrease in the maximum breathing capacity.

A decrease in physical capacity during later life is frequently the result of a deficiency in training rather than a biological necessity. It is, however, possible to change this at any age. Scientific tests have shown that even people beyond the age of 70 have the ability to undertake endurance training – and become fit.

The maximum oxygen uptake can be increased to the level of that of people twenty or thirty years younger – even at this stage of life! Cycling offers the possibility to train the heart, circulation and metabolism, and to minimise a considerable number of risk factors which, over a period of time, lead to illness in inactive people.

It is advisable for the elderly wishing to embark upon cycling initially to consult their doctor and undergo a medical examination. This should be followed by a gentle, sparing training session, perhaps with a group of recreational cyclists. This is sufficient to achieve all the desired physiological adaptations.

It is also possible to cycle competitively, even at this stage of life, if recreational cycling is not enough – and if the cyclist is one hundred per cent healthy and has trained over a period of five years. Veterans can be divided into four classes: the first class consists of cyclists of 35–45 years; cyclists aged 45–55 years belong to the second; those aged 55 to 65 to the third; and those above 65 to the fourth class of veterans. People in the third and fourth classes have to be cautioned more than the younger veterans because training and competition can be too severe in the veterans' classes. You should decide whether the motivation of veterans' races is too great, as they usually cover distances of 40–80km. The race speed is comparatively high, around 40kmh or more (these distances are comparatively short). Cycling style and tactics are slightly different from that of amateur races but the difference in performance is so slight that a race frequently finishes with a sprint and a mass finish.

Sprinting at an old age can be fairly dangerous and requires a great deal of concentration. You should decide, for example, whether you are prepared to take the risk of having a fall. It is, however, very likely that you will gain much satisfaction and pleasure from participating in these races over many years – if you have sufficient energy to do so. The cyclist remains fit and healthy into old age.

It is not possible to be successful in veterans' races without discipline throughout the year. It is important to stress at this point that competition should not be the most important part of cycling at an old age. Everyone who is able to cover long distances at a low (or average) speed by using their own power and without growing tired can count themselves lucky. Cycling at an old age conveys the feeling that you are not at the whim of the ageing process. Cycling is a genuine life enrichment and helps increase the quality of life. Cycling is a sport which can be pursued throughout your entire life.

Cycling is quite possible at an old age – as the winner of the veterans' world cup (for cyclists aged 70 or more) proves in St Johan, Austria!

Regeneration

The fundamental principle for an increased performance is the cycle of supercompensation: the regular change of training load; fatigue; regeneration (recuperation); and overcompensation. Not only is a direct adaptation gained through endurance training but also an improvement in the regeneration ability. You can noticeably improve this ability by the support of the regenerative processes.

The Meaning of Regeneration

Training loads can cause changes in the body which are interpreted as tiredness and which cause a temporary decline in performance. For the sake of simplicity, there are roughly four stages of fatigue: little; optimal; great; and extreme tiredness. The last of these needs a much longer period of regeneration than the other levels of tiredness. Two processes are set in motion by training or by races which, to some extent, occur already during the basic action of cycling.

1. The regenerative process which leads to the achievement of complete fitness and ability.
2. The adaptation process which results in an improvement to that part of the body which has been exercised.

Scientists have long been concerned with developing ways to speed up regeneration. The load endurance of cyclists would be improved through a speedier recovery – so that training could be undertaken more frequently. A new training load should, in principle, only be carried out when the most important systems of the body have fully recovered. The adaptation process is disturbed or its development hindered if you repeatedly subject a system which has not fully recovered to the

same training load. This results in permanent fatigue, the beneficial effects of the training disappear and the capacity for load endurance dwindles. The achievement of a further increase in performance from a higher level of training and more frequent training loads is not determined by the load itself but by the speed of the regenerative process. This is why it is important to be familiar with all means of regeneration and to use them all equally.

Physiological Processes

You should realise that the time needed for a single system of the body to recover varies according to the task

The face of a tired racing cyclist (Francesco Moser); deep lines on his forehead and around his mouth, hollow cheeks and dark shadows around the eyes.

it performs. There are two different types of regeneration, the fast and the slow phases.

The Fast Regeneration Phase

Lactic acid and other by-products of metabolism are broken down during the first four to six hours after a training load during which time the raised body temperature also falls and the balance of minerals and body fluids is restored. Glycogen stores are, to a large extent, renewed. The process of storing protein in the muscle fibres, however, is only just beginning. To improve regeneration you should drink plenty of fluids, minerals (particularly potassium and magnesium) and eat carbohydrate-rich foods.

The Slow Regeneration Phase

This is the phase immediately following the first six hours and lasting for the next two or three days. The glycogen stores are fully renewed during this time and the slow process of protein regeneration in the mitochondria (which require over seven days for a complete recovery) commences. The autonomic nervous system also requires four days or more to recover fully after intensive training loads (particularly important for young people). To improve regeneration you should consume carbohydrate-rich food and also as much protein as possible. Finally, you should try to be relaxed.

Regenerative Training

The entire 'system' of regeneration is made up of the following factors:

1. The correct build-up of training.
2. Correct diet.
3. Physical measures.
4. Relaxation.

Regeneration commences during the last stages of a training session and you should take this into consideration when planning your training. It is not necessary, however, to wait for complete recuperation before starting a new training session within a microcycle. The regenerative process can, in fact, be speeded up through active recuperation by carrying out training loads of lower intensity – perhaps by undertaking specific regenerative training sessions. Recovery cycles should occur regularly in all mesocycles.

A good night's sleep, a complete and suitable diet, a healthy way of life and regular 'physical measures' (including massages, restorative baths – with tonics or similar additions – daily hot and cold showers, embrocations and visits to the sauna and solarium) are all very important. Autogenic training and yoga can improve your ability to relax.

The build-up of training should go hand in hand with regeneration. Cyclists should also develop a feeling for the level of their training load and their tiredness in order to experience consciously the process of recuperation. You can only tell that you are ready for the next intensive training load when you have developed a feeling for the regenerative process. A good level of fundamental endurance is of particular

Different degrees of fatigue after different sized loads (after H. Harre)

	Slight fatigue (small load)	*Strong fatigue (optimal load)*	*Very strong fatigue (load limit)*	*Symptoms following very strong fatigue*
skin colouring	pink	red	deep red or markedly pale	continual pallor over a number of days
amount of sweat	little to medium according to temperature	large amount	very large	sweating at night
execution of movements	confident and secure	increasing number of mistakes	problems with co-ordination, movements carried out without power	movement disturbances and feebleness during the following training
concentration	normal	inattentive during explanations, decreased receptiveness when carrying out techniques and tactics	decrease in concentration, nervousness, distraction	inattentiveness, inability to correct movements, inability to concentrate on mental work
general well-being	no problems	weak in the muscles, breathing difficulties, powerlessness, decreased capacity decreased activity	muscles as heavy as lead, pain in muscles and joints, dizziness, nausea, 'burning' in the chest	disturbed sleep, restless at night, continual pain in muscles and joints, feebleness
willingness to perform	uninterrupted	desire for longer rests	desire for complete rest and the discontinuation of training	reluctance to recommence training the following day complacency, resistance against demands made by the coach
mood	happy, lively mood	a little suppressed, but generally in a happy mood	stubborn and aggressive	depressed, continual doubt about the value of training, search for excuses not to train

Regeneration

Active and passive methods of regeneration

Build-up of training	Diet	Physical measures	Relaxation
endurance	carbohydrates	massages	sleep
power	protein	baths	self-hypnosis
speed	fats	sauna	yoga
co-ordination	vitamins	(change of) climate	change of environment
(technique)	minerals and trace	altitude	surroundings with
flexibility	elements	ultra-violet rays	a positive attitude
	fluid		to sport (family, work)
			sporty way of life

importance as it improves your capacity to tolerate loads and helps your ability to recuperate.

The Day Off

Several successive training loads at the limit of a cyclist's endurance will cause exhaustion in a body which will not have completed its recovery processes. These processes are disturbed through such excessive training and the performance continues to decline. Novices frequently make this mistake because they have an insufficient fundamental endurance level and so repeatedly suffer set-backs. The training process becomes irregular, unorganised – and even a nuisance.

If this happens, there are two possible remedies: either to minimise the intensity of the training load (to train wholly within the regenerative area) or to take one or two days off following two or three such heavy training loads. Recovery can be completed in this way without interruption and the phase of overcompensation can commence. Professional racing cyclists and competitive cyclists use this 'stocking up of tiredness' consciously as a training technique in order to reach a higher level of performance after a rest day and before a more extensive demand on energy reserves. However, only competitive cyclists in good condition and with the ability to tolerate extensive loads can allow themselves to act in this way – which can sometimes produce a sudden increase in performance. A succession of heavier loads followed by a strong feeling of tiredness and a consequent decrease in performance indirectly brings about an increase in performance – when in conjunction with a rest day. Indeed a rest day seen from this point of view is sometimes quite useful for recreational cyclists who train frequently (as well as for competitive cyclists) – particularly when they feel 'empty' inside and feel a certain reluctance to train.

The phenomenon of a rest day: the regeneration gained from a rest day can lead to over-compensation after training loads with increasing fatigue – a variation in training used by many highly competitive cyclists (after H. Harre).

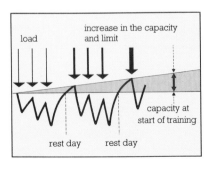

Body Care and a Healthy Lifestyle

Generally speaking, cyclists are amongst the best at looking after themselves, taking a shower after every training session being a strict rule. The skin should also be lightly oiled with, for example, baby oil. Infections or discomfort such as saddle-soreness should be avoided and it is important to wash this area thoroughly after each

training session in order to prevent inflammations or abscesses. The leather insert in the cycling shorts should always be kept clean and soft. Special cream designed to do just that is available. If you cannot find any, you can always use a similar cream containing camomile and glycerine – which should be applied before every training ride. If the leather insert has become hard after washing and drying, you should soften the insert with a little water before applying the cream.

Care (and massage) of your legs is also important. Many cyclists – and almost all racing cyclists – shave their legs as it makes it easier to massage them ('self-massage' can be quite sufficient). The use of creams and oils designed to encourage circulation should not be overdone since it promotes better circulation in the blood-vessels of the skin but not those of the muscles which lie beneath the skin. In fact the opposite is even possible – that the muscles do not have a sufficient supply of blood, because the blood supply to the skin has been increased. It is quite

sufficient to apply a thick layer of neutral oil to the skin when it is cold. (Oils containing peppermint or menthol have a cooling effect in hot conditions).

Cyclists should take every opportunity to 'toughen' their body because they will have to face all kinds of weather. They should be able to tolerate wet, windy, cold or hot weather and should be comfortable training outside during the winter – not only on the home-trainer.

Cold water, in the form of an early morning shower, also helps strengthen the body. It has been proven beneficial to massage the entire body with a coarse brush starting at the extremities and working towards the heart – until the skin is completely red. This increases the body's resistance against infection. In summary, a cyclist's body needs just as much care and attention as his bicycle.

If you hope to achieve significant success in cycling, the experience of world-class racing cyclists – who have built up their great performances not only through regular, purposeful training over a considerable number of years but also through living a sports-orientated way of life – cannot be ignored. Cyclists who smoke, drink alcohol and do not manage enough sleep will never be very successful in the long run, even if they train extensively. Sensible habits involving a daily routine, correct diet, sufficient sleep and the abstinence from all factors which minimise an athlete's performance must form part of a sports-orientated way of life. Every means of helping regeneration should always be encouraged so that the benefits of training are brought to bear on a body which can incorporate these effects as efficiently as possible.

Experienced competitive cyclists who have dominated numerous races for many years (from the right: Freddy Maertens, Walter Goodefrot, Garry Knetemann).

Diet

Scientific research has made a number of new discoveries over the past few years so far as the influence of diet on health and fitness is concerned. Within the body nourishment has the following three objectives:

1. The construction and preservation of cells and tissues.
2. The regulation of the metabolism and the construction of enzymes.
3. The supply of energy.

Protein is predominantly used for the construction of cells and tissues while carbohydrates and fats are responsible for the energy supply. Vitamins, minerals and trace elements allow optimal metabolism to take place. Fluid is also vital for all metabolic processes.

Diet Balances

A diet designed to promote performance will fulfil all the actual requirements of the body and be sufficiently complete to allow the following balances to be levelled:

1. The energy balance.
2. The nutrient balance.
3. The vitamin balance.
4. The balance of minerals and trace elements.
5. The fluid balance.

The food intake needs to be varied since there is no single food which can supply the body with all its needs. Competitive cyclists should consume highly nutritious types of food and should bear in mind that there are many highly processed foods on the market today which no longer contain nutrients to their original density because the composition has been artificially changed. The foodstuffs of the modern diet are known as 'empty calories'. The first step towards a healthy performance diet is taken by avoiding these unsatisfactory foods (see the table below). The second step is to choose many highly nutritious foods which have the correct nutritional composition, preferably exactly suited to your individual needs.

'Empty calories' – poor nourishment for cyclists

sugar, foods and drinks containing sugar
monosaccharides (glucose)   disaccharides (cane-sugar, beet-sugar)   sweets (confectionery, chocolate, nougat, jam, marmalade, gateaux)   drinks containing sugar   (lemonade, Coke)
Products made with strongly processed flour (white-flour products)   white bread, rolls, toast, cakes, biscuits and similar
Strongly processed rice
Fat, foods with a high fat content and those prepared with large amounts of fat.   fried foods (such as chops)   noodles pancakes sausages,   fatty bacon and ham   egg yolk (fat and cholesterol!) and others
Alcohol

Average energy requirement per day per kilogram of body-weight

category	kcal	kJ
health-related sport	40–50	170–210
competitive sport	60–70	250–290
very competitive sport	70–80	290–340

Grain, wheatgerm, dried fruit, milk and fruit. These form the most important fundamental nourishment for cyclists.

Diet

Use of energy during one hour's training – depending upon performance category and training intensity

category	maximum intake of oxygen (l/min)*	training intensity level			
		I	II	III	IV
health-related sport	2–4	240–480	360–720	420–840	— **
competitive sport	4–5	480–600	720–900	840–1050	960–1200
very competitive sport	5–6	600–720	900–1080	1050–1260	1200–1440

* estimated average values
** intensity level four and above are not applicable to popular/health-related sports

Energy Balance

Performance sport is minimised through under- as well as over-eating. The energy consumption of cyclists is greater the longer and particularly the more intensively they train. The amount of energy used is in proportion to the amount of the oxygen used. For every litre of oxygen, 5kcal (21kJ) of energy are generated. The deciding factor for energy consumption is the intensity of training, so recreational cyclists use around 500–800kcal (2,100–3,300kJ) per hour – certainly no more. Competitive cyclists, however, use around 1,200–1,500kcal (5,000–6,300kJ) an hour during intensive training or in a race. This means that a cyclist will have an energy consumption of 5,000–7,500kcal (21,000–31,500kJ) in a race lasting between four and six hours – far more than is consumed by recreational cyclists. The average daily energy requirement for a recreational cyclist is 2,500–3,500kcal (10,500–14,700kJ) and usually more than 5,000kcal (21,000kJ) for competitive cyclists.

The energy balance is best checked by regularly controlling your body-weight; if your body-weight remains constant over a long period of time then your energy balance is level. The ideal is your competition weight – the weight at which you enjoy the majority of your successes (and which competitive cyclists can usually only maintain for a short period of time).

Nutritional Balance

The normal Western diet does not form a good basis upon which to build a healthy diet to prepare you for strenuous exercise. The amount of carbohydrate can form as little as 35 per cent of the calorie intake. This needs to be raised to at least 50–60 per cent of the calories – and 'empty' carbohydrates should be replaced with nutritious carbohydrates in order to avoid vitamin and mineral deficiency. The level of protein is almost sufficient at 12kcal%. It should, however, be raised to 15kcal% and you should choose proteins which are both biologically valuable and low in fat.

The high fat content (40–45kcal%) of the Western diet is the worst enemy of an increase in performance; foodstuffs with a high fat content markedly minimise your performance. Accordingly, the fat intake should be drastically cut down, preferably to 30kcal% or less.

On average the intake of alcohol forms 10 per cent of the normal Western diet. Alcohol, in fact, has no place at all within an athlete's diet because it hinders their regenerative ability. A reduction in the levels of sex hormones in the bloodstream can be detected if 30g of pure alcohol is consumed per day. This should therefore form the absolute limit for the consumption of alcohol. (One litre of beer or 0.375l of wine contain about 30g of alcohol.)

Carbohydrates

The most important energy supply for endurance loads are carbohydrates – from which the body also builds up its carbohydrate stores (muscle and liver glycogen). Carbohydrates are also important because they supply vitamins (B-complex in particular), minerals, trace elements and roughage. The fact that six of the twenty-four atoms that make up a carbohydrate molecule are oxygen atoms (twenty-five per cent) is very important to athletes – whose maximum endurance speed is limited by their maximum oxygen uptake. Carbohydrates and carbohydrate stores gain further significance as the intensity of the load increases; in other words, they are particularly important for all competitive cyclists.

Valuable nourishment with a high carbohydrate content

Wholemeal and wholemeal products: wholemeal bread, wholemeal biscuits (oat biscuits), breakfast cereals (oats, wheatflakes, millet, corn flakes)
brown rice
potatoes
fruit, fruit juice, dried fruit
pulses (peas, beans, lentils)
To improve the goodness of less valuable carbohydrates: wheatgerm, yeast tablets, brewer's yeast

Diet

Valuable fats and oils

fish oil in mackerel, herring and salmon
sunflower oil, maize oil, soya oil, linseed oil
butter

Fats

When discussing fats and the metabolism of fat, two points must be taken into consideration.

1.   An athlete's diet should be low in fat because performance is impaired by fat. Hence foodstuffs which may or may not have the appearance of fatty foods, but which have a high fat content should be kept to a minimum. You should only consume small amounts of fats and oils and those which are consumed should be valuable fats which supply the body with the necessary fatty acids (see the relevant table for more details).

2.   The fat metabolism must be trained because it is the biochemical basis for a good fundamental endurance. Only those who have improved their fat metabolism with intense aerobic training (a low-to-medium intensity and high quantity) can utilise this high quality and inexhaustible energy reserve – and so save the valuable and limited carbohydrates (oxygen-rich energy carriers) for intensive performances.

Proteins

Proteins act predominantly as construction material – particularly for muscle fibres, enzymes and hormones. Cyclists use about twice as much protein after intensive cycling as they do normally (around 1.5–2.5g protein per kilogram of body-weight). This protein should be of 'high quality' biologically in order to produce as little fat as possible as a by-product – and so proteins with a low fat content are preferable and the biological value of these proteins is increased.

Vitamin Balance

Endurance athletes consume considerable amounts of the vitamin B complex (B1, B2, B6, B12) as well as vitamins C and E. Consuming insufficient amounts of these vitamins gives rise to poor performance and perhaps illness, and so cyclists should be familiar with those foodstuffs that are rich in these vitamins.

Valuable nourishment rich in proteins and low in fat

Low-fat milk and low-fat milk products: skimmed milk, yoghurt, cheese, cottage cheese, curd cheese,
Low-fat fish: cod, flounder, plaice, sole, trout, mackerel, salmon, herring
low-fat meat: chicken, beef, veal, hare, venison and other game
egg-white (the yolk contains considerable fat)
Pulses: peas, beans, soya beans, lentils

Note: the increase in value of building proteins extends over four to six hours, so that these convenient protein combinations need not be taken simultaneously, but can be distributed over a period of time.

Advantageous combinations of nourishment with additional protein

Cereal or cereal products with milk or with pulses or with eggs
Potatoes with egg or with milk or milk products

Foods with high content of vitamin B_1 and B_2

wheatgerm, oats, brewer's yeast
wholewheat and wholewheat products
cereals
brown rice
meat, heart, liver
egg yolk

Foods with a high vitamin C content

cherries, rose-hips
oranges, satsumas, grapefruit, lemons, kiwi-fruit
berries (black currants, strawberries and others, fruit and fruit juices (citrus-fruit juices, blackcurrant juice, grape juice, apple juice and others)
vegetables (broccoli, kale and similar)
lettuce
potatoes
parsley
horseradish
capsicum

Foods with a high vitamin E content

oils (wheat oil, maize oil, soya oil)
grain (wheatgerm, soya germ and others)
soya beans, peas
nuts
wholewheat and wholewheat products
cereal
brown rice

Drinking is more important than eating during a cycle race in hot weather.

Diet

The Balance of Minerals and Trace Elements

Need is predominantly governed by the amount of loss through sweating. In athletes this can rise to twice or three times the usual amount. The loss of sodium chloride (salt) is usually ade-

Foods with a high potassium content

beef extract, tomato puree, cocoa powder
dried fruits (apricots, figs, raisins, plums and others)
potatoes
fruit (bananas, apricots, avocado and others)
vegetables (tomatoes, fennel, spinach and others)
pulses (white beans, peas, lentils)
brewer's yeast
nuts (pistachio, almonds, hazelnuts and others)

Foods with a high magnesium content

cocoa powder, beef extract, brewer's yeast
nuts (peanuts, peanut butter, hazelnuts, cashew nuts, almonds, marzipan and others)
pulses (soya beans, peas and others)
brown rice
wholewheat and wholewheat products
cereals (oats, corn flakes and others)
wheatgerm
fish (mackerel, trout and others)
meat (beef, veal and others)
cheese (Edam, Gouda)

Foods with a high iron content

liver
pulses (soya beans, lentils, haricot beans)
nuts (pistachio, sunflower seeds, hazelnuts, almonds)
millet, wheatgerm, oats
brewer's yeast
cocoa powder
parsley, spinach, cress
dried fruit (apricots, figs)
wholewheat and wholewheat products
meat (beef, veal and others)

Foods with a high selenium content

sesame seeds, wheatgerm
wholewheat oats
mushrooms
molasses
eggs
fish, fish oil
liver
dates
asparagus

After a race cyclists should replace lost fluid gradually.

quately replaced through the normal Western diet but it is more difficult to replace lost potassium, magnesium and iron through the normal diet. Potassium is stored in the muscle cells with the carbohydrate (glycogen) and must be absorbed at the same time. Another important trace element for the athlete's oxidative metabolism seems to be selenium.

The Fluid Balance

It is very important for competitive cyclists to realise that a loss of fluid will always occur at the same time as a loss

of minerals and trace elements. Cyclists should therefore replace lost fluid and lost minerals at the same time.

Fluid losses of as little as two per cent of the body-weight (1.4l for a weight of 70kg) reduces the endurance capacity while a fluid loss of four per cent of the body-weight (2.8l) reduces the power capacity. The mistake of replacing lost fluid with mineral-free drinks such as lemonade, coca-cola and tea is frequently made; this can lead to a mineral-deficiency syndrome with tiredness, a reluctance to exercise and muscle cramps. Even so-called mineral waters contain only small amounts of minerals which are usually insufficient to replace the minerals lost through sweating.

Fruit and fruit juices, however, supply the body with plenty of potassium and magnesium as well as fluid. A very good drink which has been tried and tested in the world of cycling is a mixture of apple juice and mineral water in equal quantities. Another option is to eat dried fruits such as apricots, figs and raisins, all of which contain large amounts of minerals and trace elements. Specifically formulated energy drinks are another very good solution.

Diet Phases

There are several different phases of your diet which need to be understood before they can be integrated with your training:

1. The phase of building up training.
2. The pre-competition phase.
3. The competition phase.
4. The post-competition phase.

Several points must be made to ensure that the diet is adequate and corresponds to the cyclist's needs.

The Training Phase

Cyclists who train for fundamental endurance during the preparation stage of training and wish to improve their ability to metabolise fat will increase the effects of their training if their intake of food is quite small. The less food you eat, however, the more nutritious foodstuffs must be in order to avoid deficiencies of any kind. At this stage you should also cause your body to burn up stores of fat and so lose weight since the maximum oxygen uptake increases per kilogram of body-weight – even through weight loss alone. Food and drinks with a high sugar content as well as alcohol should be avoided. Cyclists should construct their diet from the following items during both the second stage of the preparation phase and the competition phase.

1. Foods with a high carbohydrate content, consisting mainly of polysaccharides (starch), and which also contain those vitamins, minerals and trace elements necessary for the metabolism of the carbohydrates.
2. Foods with a high protein content, of good 'biological quality,' low in fat.
3. Small amounts of fats of high quality particularly high in unsaturated fatty acids.
4. Vegetables, fruit, dried fruit and fruit juices with a large amount of vitamins, minerals and trace elements.

Finally, here is a summary of the basic rules converning a simple diet:

1. Always remember the foodstuffs with a low fat content.
2. Raise the carbohydrate level in the diet before and after intensive endurance loads.

Remember: only use dried fruits that do not contain sulphur because sulphur dioxide – used for the preservation of these products – can counteract important enzymes, destroy vitamin B1 and cause headaches in some people.

Summary of the most valuable foods

Corn: wholemeal products (bread, rice), rolled oats, millet
Fruits: bananas, apples, citrus fruits, dried fruits (apricots, figs, raisins)
Nuts and seeds: hazelnuts, sunflower seeds, pistachio, almonds, sesame seeds
Juices: apple juice, citrus-fruit juices, grape juice, black currant juice
Milk and milk products: yoghurt, milk, cheese, curd cheese
Fish: mackerel, herring, salmon, trout, plaice and others
To increase the nutrition of less valuable food: soya germ, wheatgerm, yeast, yeast tablets, brewer's yeast, cocoa powder, pollen, meat extract

3. Raise the protein level during the period of regeneration.
4. Replace lost fluid with fruit juices, if at all possible, or with fruits with a high water content (such as apples or oranges) or with dried fruits combined with fluid.

The Pre-competition Phase

The economical, oxygen-rich carbohydrate reserves of the body (muscle and liver glycogen) should be built up three or four days before a race; you should use the fundamental principle of overcompensation for this purpose. You should carry out a training session three or four days before the race which is of the right quantity and intensity to empty the glycogen reserves. You should follow this by consuming generous quantities of those foods which have a high carbohydrate content. The body reacts by building up a stock of glycogen during the regeneration process which is larger than it would have been without this glycogen-emptying training load. So you can see that training and diet are always closely linked.

The Competition Phase

On the day of the race it is important to use the developed capacity without disruption and so it is vital that you should make no mistakes at this stage of preparation – not even in your diet. You should most certainly not change to unfamiliar or new diets and you should be aware of those foods which should be consumed before the race and those which should be consumed during the race.

What to Eat before a Race

The last meal before a race should be eaten one and a half or two hours before long races (perhaps lasting all

Diet

How long different types of food stay in the stomach

Duration in the stomach	Foodstuffs
1–2 hours	water, coffee, tea, cocoa, thin soup, beer, soft-boiled eggs, cooked rice, fresh-water fish
2–3 hours	boiled milk, coffee with cream, cocoa with milk, potatoes, mashed potato, cooked vegetables, fruit, white bread, raw eggs, hard-boiled eggs, scrambled eggs, omelette, salt- water fish, veal
3–4 hours	wholemeal bread, fried potatoes, swede, turnips, radishes, spinach, cucumber salad, apples, roast veal, beef steak (raw or cooked), ham, cooked young chicken
4–5 hours	pulses, string beans, fried chicken and game, smoked meat, fillet of venison (fried), salted herrings
6–7 hours	bacon, herrings, mushrooms
7–8 hours	roast duck, sardines (in oil)

day) and two or three hours before the start of short races. This last meal can be quite normal (perhaps a grilled, lean piece of steak of about 200g with potatoes or rice and a little salad) because the glycogen stocks have already been filled. Some cyclists eat muesli before the start of a race while others prefer a raw steak! You should, however, not fill yourself up but eat only so much that you still feel slightly hungry. You should also choose foods which do not stay in the stomach for a long time and are easily digestible.

What to Eat and Drink during a Race

Every road-racing cyclist, in principle, should be able to complete a cycle race without much food intake during the race. An appropriate fundamental endurance training (which means an optimal training of the fat metabolism as well as the stocking up of good quality carbohydrates during the period before the race) makes a long endurance performance without a large intake of food quite possible. Food, however, is advisable when participating in road or day races which cover distances in excess of 80km. You should have some food one or two hours after the start of the race. The following items have

been shown to be rich in carbohydrates and so suitable for consumption during a race; bananas, fruit cake, dried fruit, rice cake, cereal bars, oat biscuits, apple slices and orange segments.

These types of food are particularly important during cold training sessions, during mountain-pass cycling and during the first long races of the season. You should also carry a form of concentrated nutritious fluid in a bottle which should contain carbohydrates as well as minerals. These mixtures are particularly welcome (and important) in hot conditions because you can easily lose 1.5–2l in an hour. Fluid deficiency raises the body temperature, decreases the performance and increases the possibility of cramp arising

Jersey pockets should contain sensible nourishment during long cycle rides.

from a deficiency of minerals. You should, however, discipline yourself to take only small amounts of food during racing because the bent, cycling position does not leave much room in the stomach and can have an adverse effect on breathing and the development of performance.

The Post-race Phase

It is not always possible to meet fully every need through race provisions and the intake of fluid. A fluid deficit of around 3–4l may sometimes remain after hard races – despite fluid intake during races – which can be recognised by a loss in weight. The resulting thirst should be quenched slowly after the race and preferably not by cold drinks, because the stomach and intestines are particularly vulnerable. The first meal after the race – and also after training loads – should be taken after the finish of the race or training session. It should be rich in carbohydrates and proteins and have a low fat content. The fluid level should be levelled out gently over the next few hours.

Nutrient Concentrates

These can make up for deficiencies in an athlete's diet; they should never be a substitute for a healthy basic diet but rather supplement it. The most suitable of these concentrates are mixtures of minerals and carbohydrates, protein preparations (usually milk and/or soya protein) as well as regeneration concentrates which contain equal amounts of carbohydrates, protein, minerals and vitamins. The sensible and sparing consumption of nutrient supplements depends upon the need which will have arisen through training or race loads.

Competition Racing Programme

Racing cyclists, unlike athletes of different endurance sports, have always had to participate in a large number of competitions. Cyclists from some countries such as Belgium may ride two or three races a week! A high competition frequency does not decrease a cyclist's form – on the contrary, practice has often proved that a series of races (such as a stage race) is a good way to prepare highly trained cyclists for the climax of the season – national or world championships. The frequency of participation in competitions can increase with the years of cycling. The planning of competitions forms part of a year's programme.

Physical Preparation for Competition

The quantity of training within a mesocycle is greatly reduced. The foundation for intensive race loads should be built up from long, fitness-promoting training. Some cyclists improve their race speed one or two weeks before a race by practising a series of sprints or by undertaking short-term interval-training in order to increase both their aerobic capacity and the number of energy-rich phosphates within their muscles. Cyclists usually cycle in a relaxed, easy manner during the last two or three days before a race.

Races require complete physical and mental effort.

Competition

Mental Preparation for Competition

All training loads exercise both the mental and physical capacity of the cyclist. A strong 'performance drive', a positive attitude towards racing, plenty of self-confidence and self-awareness are also necessary for success. The mental attitude to the coming race undoubtedly affects how prepared you are to perform well – the body should be 'programmed' to perform. You can prepare yourself for the coming race by imagining the race situations you will encounter. In your mind you can repeatedly go over tactics and strategies that you will use at certain points in the race – so that it is easier for you to turn these into reality on the day of the race. Positive thinking and visualis-

ing tactics are valuable mental techniques.

The Day of the Race

Most cycle races begin early in the morning perhaps between seven and eight o'clock. This is why the 'race day' really starts on the previous day when you should consume foods rich in carbohydrates and go to bed early. You should then get up at least three or four hours before the start because your body needs time to prepare itself before it is ready to perform. Take your usual breakfast after the normal routine of washing and early-morning exercises and cycle for a while in order to

warm up. It is common practice to reach the start about an hour before the race in order to collect your race number and fasten it to your jersey.

Other preparations such as massage, oiling of the legs, an inspection of the bicycle, a check on the food to be consumed during the race, the contents of the bottle and so forth are also necessary and should be carried out when there is still plenty of time – and not at the last moment. The actual warming-up procedure should commence thirty or forty minutes before the race.

A little nervousness and some hectic jostling is quite common during the first minutes after the start, particularly in the less experienced categories or in the veterans' event. You should face these symptoms with calmness and concentration.

The start of a time trial: this discipline requires special effort – both mental and physical.

Strategy and Tactics

This cannot be considered in detail due to lack of space, but some fundamental principles will be mentioned.

The route should be examined before a race, and you should select the gears in which you are going to ride. You should always cycle in as low a gear as possible so that the perfect, round pedal action can be maintained in a relaxed fashion. This is the only way in which you will be able to keep up with a sudden change in speed.

You should always try to cycle within the first third of a group of cyclists as this is the only way to recognise how the race is developing and it also gives you the best opportunity to react to attacks. The speed also tends to be less erratic at the front than at the back, where acceleration and deceleration occur frequently because of the 'concertina-effect'.

You should always attempt to ride in the first group of cyclists if 'echelons' are formed to combat the effects of the wind – otherwise you will waste energy or even fall back. If the cyclists in the first echelon co-operate, they may even be able to shake off the other cyclists in a situation like this.

Good cyclists ride actively as far as their powers permit them. If you want to be successful, you must be prepared to attack – on your own as well as with another rider. A racing cyclist also needs the courage to push ahead and break away, but these actions must be carefully considered because failed attempts of this kind waste valuable energy. It is always best to make a move when it is unlikely that other cyclists will do so – for instance because they are tired.

An attack should be ridden in the following way: change into a sprint gear, move out into the wind edge and ride ten or fifteen metres in front of the echelon so that no other cyclist can follow in your slipstream. The first kilometre or so is ridden at a very high speed without turning your head. Only now can you look around to determine whether the break was successful. You change down, take a deep breath and fall back into the first echelon if the attempt was not successful, resolving to repeat the attempt at the next opportunity – and again until it is successful, preferably with the help of another cyclist with the same aim.

You should start a regular intake of food after the first hour of cycling, but not just before climbs or when riding in the front of a bunch or at the front of the race.

Hills must always be climbed with great power and concentration because the majority of attempts to break away are made here – usually on the last third of a hill or at the top.

You must prepare yourself for the finishing sprint at a mass finish. This should be done by attempting to ride with ten or fifteen riders in front of you during the last few kilometres of the race. About one kilometre from the finish you should decide upon the most favourable position for a sprint finish.

Both cyclists try to cover the last few centimetres before the finish as quickly as possible by 'throwing their machines'.

For this you ride in the slipstream of the cyclist in front but only so close that there is enough lateral room for overtaking. Every finishing sprint is different and so tactics change according to the situation. (Pushing the handlebars over the finishing line is quite common.)

There are, of course, more basic tactics involved in road racing, but these are probably the most important. Practice makes perfect as always; you will need to participate in many races and learn from your experience.

Competition

After the Race

The development of a race and its subsequent finish strongly affect the cyclist both mentally and physiologically. Winners are exhilarated and fresh, losers and all those who are disappointed are weak, tired and irritable. The load was roughly the same for everyone (possibly even heavier for the winners than the losers) – but the winners are, of course, much fresher than the losers.

This is a common experience in every sports discipline and certain proof of the psychological effect of competition. Coaches and friends should ignore these moods; cyclists should not become involved in lengthy discussions, but simply do what has to be done – hand in the race number, take a shower, eat and drink. They should be disciplined to drink slowly and to avoid cold drinks because the intestines and the stomach are particularly vulnerable immediately following a race. A light meal rich in carbohydrates and proteins will, once again, aid the transition to the training build-up phase. Mental 'regeneration' will be promoted by active recuperation and regenerative training sessions.

Not everyone can be a star like Claude Criquielion (left) and Greg Lemond (centre), of course. Nevertheless we do somehow try to emulate the professional cyclists, each according to their own ability.

Cycling and Medicine

Cycling is an ideal alternative to jogging if you are hoping to stabilise your health through exercise, prevent disease or cope with existing disease through active long-term therapy and therapeutic sport.

The Medical Check-up

Everyone who wishes to embark upon training after the age of 35 should undergo a medical check-up. This will include an examination of certain risk factors (such as blood pressure and blood tests) checking for those illnesses whcih would prohibit physical exercise and perhaps electrocardiography. Such examinations can be carried out by any general practitioner.

Cycling as Therapy

The incidence of chronic disease is increasing. Acute illness, untreatable only a few years ago, may often nowadays be 'cured'.

The result, however, is that many people suffer from the after-effects of an illness from which they have not completely recovered – in other words, they are chronically ill. Experience has shown that many can be helped through a long-term, active programme of sport – such as cycling.

Contra-indications against Physical Exercise

There are, in principle, few 'contra-indications' which prevent you from taking even a small dose of properly-controlled physical therapy. Those that do exist are, basically; too high blood pressure, dangerous heart-rhythm disorders, too low a capacity (less than one Watt per kilogram of bodyweight), disorders of a high degree which have arisen from the original illness, and acute infections.

Cycling as an Active, Long-term Therapy

Sport has been proved and tested as therapeutic to varying degrees for the following diseases: disorders of the coronary blood-vessels; for recovery after heart attacks; for high and low blood pressure: circulatory disturbances; vein disorders; bronchial asthma and chronic bronchitis; metabolism disorders (diabetes, obesity, gout); for disorders of the motor system and the spine (arthritis and rheumatism); as well as for psychiatric-neurological disorders (disturbances of the autonomic nervous system, psychosomatic illnesses, neurosis, depression, dependencies on medication, alcohol and drugs); and finally for the improvement of geriatric diseases even at an advanced age, as well as the promotion of the mental and physical development of children and youth.

How much Cycling?

The guidelines for training given earlier are designed for those in good health. The yardstick of using your pulse is not suitable for people who are not well, who are elderly or who take medication to slow down their heart rate. The following simple, fundamental rule is suitable for these people; work only so hard that you can still utter a complete sentence without becoming breathless.

Complaints during Cycling

In spite of its powerful health-maintaining and therapeutic effects, complaints can arise during cycling. These complaints can usually be traced back to incorrect training or an incorrect strain on the body. Some examples are: over-training, complaints caused by the abrupt finish of a training session, saddle-soreness or similar problems, muscle cramp, back problems, headaches caused by a strong oncoming wind, knee complaints, hand and lower arm complaints – as well as colds.

Saddle-soreness

Cyclists actually sit on the saddle with their pelvic bones. You will notice pressure pains in this area in the beginning, but these soon disappear. You should realise that these complaints are quite normal – and that the saddle is not to blame. Cyclists who cover long distances make a greater demand upon this area of the body and so hygiene and care are required. Soreness and boils can be prevented by cycling in cycle shorts with a leather insert. A special cream should be applied to the insert before every cycle ride.

Muscle Cramp

Cramp occurs for a number of reasons and is most frequent in the region of the calves. The most common cause is a mineral deficiency – particularly of magnesium and potassium – which can occur after prolonged sweating, especially when you have not rigidly adhered to the correct diet. Another reason could be the use of too high or too low gears. The sitting position should be correct if cramp is to be avoided.

Backache

Cyclists who train on racing bicycles may suffer from aches in the lower region of their back. This is usually caused by muscle tension, displacements of the small joints of the spine or too much strain on the joints of the lower back. Exposure may also be the reason for aching bones. These complaints can be treated by a number of different methods, the most important of which is a regular routine of spine exercises. Yoga is also advisable. You should check your position on the racing bicycle, ensuring that you cycle in as relaxed a fashion as possible, predominantly using the upper position of the handlebars and taking every opportunity to stand up on the pedals. Warmth-giving paraphernalia such as mudpacks and embrocations can be used for complaints caused by exposure. You could also wear a rheumatism 'plaster' during training. Your diet should be checked and too many meat dishes avoided with an increase in the intake of lactic-vegetarian foods.

Neck Complaints

Tension in the neck muscles can arise through an incorrect, cramped position on the bicycle, perhaps leaning too far forward. Your position must be correct; the level of the handlebars should not be much lower than the saddle. Your cycling style should be noticeably relaxed and the top position of the handlebars should be predominantly used. Cyclists who are able to do so should, during a training session, cycle sitting upright (without holding on to the bicycle) and shake their arms and relax their neck and shoulders. A daily routine of spine exercises should ideally be carried out every morning in order to prevent and/or cure these complaints.

Headaches

Headaches can be caused by tension in the neck muscles. Headaches which are caused by exposure to the cold wind are, however, more common. This is frequently the case when a cyclist reaches the top of a hill and is sweating heavily from the climb. The wind which buffets the cyclist during the descent and the evaporating sweat on the cyclist's forehead are so cooling that this can cause severe headaches. Wearing a cycle cap easily prevents this.

Knee Complaints

Cycling is very gentle on the joints. Knee complaints can, however, arise although they probably have nothing to do with the actual knee joint. These are usually strains of the kneecap, the base of the tendons under the kneecap, and of the bursa in front of the kneecap. These strains are caused by cycling in too high a gear and in cold winds, particularly during the spring. You must always 'break in' these parts of your knee by gentle training. You should cycle in lower gears, minimise the lever effect of the kneecap and tendons by cycling in a standing position (and protect your knees from the cold by wearing long leggings if you already suffer from these complaints). A change in your sitting position can also cause knee complaints; this is sometimes the case with racing cyclists who ride time-trialling machines during stage races — as these are different from their usual racing bicycles.

Numerous complaints can be caused by an incorrect sitting position.

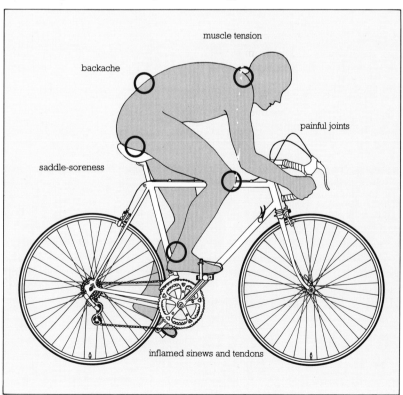

Cycling and Medicine

Hand and Lower Arm Complaints

Great demand is, from time to time, made upon the muscles of the lower arm, especially when handlebars are held tightly. This is why your grip on the handlebars should be loosened occasionally. Otherwise it is possible for cyclists to suffer a form of 'tennis elbow' – on both arms – because the pull of the tendons on the elbow is constantly too strong. Pressure lesions from the nerves of the wrists will often occur if you lean upon the handlebars with your wrists (numb fingers are a symptom of these lesions). This is another reason why you should change the grip on the handlebars and why you should not lean on one part of them too heavily. The hands should also be frequently removed from the handlebars and relaxed.

Colds

Cyclists have to cope with more severe weather conditions than most other athletes because the wind which is created during cycling exacerbates these conditions. They are often caught in cold and rainy weather (particularly in the spring) and sometimes even in blizzards. Cyclists must be prepared for these changes in the weather because they may result in their catching a cold. It is very important to maintain an athletic way of life so that the body is always encouraged to recover (or regenerate).

Cyclists should undertake every possible 'toughening' procedure; they should take alternate hot and cold showers – finishing with a cold shower – or have a cold wash in the morning. Washing after training should also end with a cold shower (the blood-vessels of the skin are exercised by this procedure). Another effective means of toughening up is to have a sauna. The correct clothing is also important when cycling. It is sometimes quite frightening to see how cyclists sin against this rule! Wind and rain are the two worst enemies of the cyclist because these cool you down very quickly; it is therefore important to use thermal or waterproof clothing and you should always wear a woolly hat during the winter as a significant amount of heat is lost from the head. A good supply of vitamins is also essential for the body to develop resistance; this means a well-balanced diet with plenty of fruit and vegetables. And finally, the very training loads themselves strengthen the immune system of the body.

You can enjoy nature and all the glory of the countryside as a recreational cyclist.

Cycling and Medicine

Cycling as a Health and Leisure Sport

Lack of exercise contributes greatly to the various causes of disease in our modern society. There is no doubt about the importance and necessity of a certain level of physical exercise. The sedentary lifestyle of today is, of course, unhealthy. There is no need to take part in competitions in order to arrest the harm brought about by lack of exercise, but some minimal loads of exercise are necessary to maintain a healthy body. Sports disciplines which build up endurance are particularly effective. Cycling is unusual in this field because the body-weight is carried by the saddle.

A sufficient adaptation of the heart, circulation and metabolism can be achieved without too much strain on the movement apparatus. Cycling is suitable for all ages, if practised sensibly. The advantage of cycling is that it has a strengthening effect on the immune system when pursued in fresh air. Cycling as a regenerative and leisure sport diminishes nervous tension and can aid us all in the prevention of illness. Everyone who enjoys cycling has the opportunity to build it into a social activity; it is quite possible to participate in cycling in large groups or you could join a racing club.

The many different aspects of cycling can be explored through clubs and by forming groups. The addresses of the most important clubs and groups are given below.

Useful Addresses

British Cycling Federation
36 Rockingham Road
Kettering
Northamptonshire
NN16 8HG
0536 412211

British Cyclo-Cross Association
59 Jordan Road
Sutton Coldfield
West Midlands
B75 5AE
021 308 1246

Cycle Speedway Council
57 Rectory Lane
Poringland
Norwich
NR14 7SW
05086 3880

Cyclists' Touring Club
Cotterell House
69 Meadrow
Godalming
Surrey
GU7 7HS
04868 7217/8

Road Time Trials Council
Dallacre
Mill Road
Yarwell
Peterborough
Cambridgeshire
PE8 6PS
0780 782464

Postscript

This book aims to show that everyone can participate in cycling, whether male or female, young or old, of high or low ability. Those who cycle regularly have found a means of developing both mentally and physically, and of enriching their lives. This is why the bicycle is such an excellent piece of sports equipment – it sets us tasks which, in their achievement, help to develop and fulfil us. Those who wish to penetrate further the secrets of cycling, or who are already familiar with the ups and downs of the cyclist's life will already be fascinated by it, and will be unable to free themselves from its grasp. They will always cycle out into nature and will remain healthy, maintain their fitness and stay mentally alert – even into old age!

Conversion Tables

Length

mm (millimetres)	inches
1	0.039
2	0.079
3	0.118
4	0.157
5	0.197
6	0.236
7	0.276
8	0.315
9	0.354
10	0.394
20	0.787
30	1.181
40	1.575
50	1.968
60	2.362
70	2.756
80	3.150
90	3.543
100	3.937

m (metres)	yards
1	1.094
2	2.187
3	3.281
4	4.374
5	5.468
6	6.562
7	6.655
8	8.749
9	9.842
10	10.937
20	21.872
30	32.808
40	43.744
50	54.680
60	65.616
70	76.552
80	87.488
90	98.424
100	109.360

km (kilometres)	miles
1	0.621
2	1.243
3	1.864
4	2.485
5	3.107
6	3.728
7	4.350
8	4.971
9	5.592
10	6.214
20	12.427
30	18.641
40	24.855
50	31.069
60	37.282
70	43.496
80	49.710
90	55.923
100	62.137

Volume

ml (milliletres)	fl oz (fluid ounces)
1	0.035
2	0.070
3	0.106
4	0.141
5	0.176
6	0.211
7	0.246
8	0.282
9	0.317
10	0.352
20	0.704
30	1.056
40	1.408
50	1.760
60	2.112
70	2.464
80	2.816
90	3.167
100	3.519

1000ml A 1l A 35.194fl oz A 1.760pts A 0.220 UK gallons

l (litres)	UK gallons
1	0.220
2	0.440
3	0.660
4	0.880
5	1.110
6	1.320
7	1.540
8	1.760
9	1.980
10	2.200
20	4.399
30	6.599
40	8.799
50	10.998
60	13.198
70	15.398
80	17.598
90	19.797
100	21.997

Weight

g (grams)	oz (ounces)
1	0.035
2	0.071
3	0.141
4	0.106
5	0.176
6	0.212
7	0.247
8	0.282
9	0.317
10	0.353
20	0.705
30	1.058
40	1.411
50	1.764
60	2.116
70	2.470
80	2.822
90	3.175
100	3.527

kg (kilograms)	lbs (pounds)
1	2.205
2	4.409
3	6.614
4	8.819
5	11.023
6	13.228
7	15.432
8	17.637
9	19.842
10	22.046
20	44.092
30	66.139
40	88.185
50	110.231
60	132.277
70	154.324
80	176.370
90	198.416
100	220.462

Shoe Sizes

European	38	38	39	39	40	41	42	42	43	43	44	45	45	46
British	4½	5	5½	6	6½	7	7½	8	8½	9	9½	10	10½	11
American	women's shoes – add 1½ to British measurement; men's – add 1													

Index

Index